A COMPENDIUM

OF

𝕻𝖗𝖆𝖈𝖙𝖎𝖈𝖆𝖑 𝕸𝖚𝖘𝖎𝖈𝖐

IN FIVE PARTS.

Teaching, by a New, and easie Method,

1. *The Rudiments of Song.*
2. *The Principles of Composition.*
3. *The Use of Discords.*
4. *The Form of Figurate Descant.*
5. *The Contrivance of Canon.*

Together with

LESSONS for VIOLS, &c.

The Third Editio.

By *CHRISTOPHER SIMPSON.*

PSAL. cxlix.

Cantate Domino Canticum novum.
Laus ejus in Ecclesia Sanctorum.

LONDON,
Printed by *M.C.* for *Henry Brome,* at the
Gun near the West-end of St. *Pauls.*
M DC LXXVIII.

Christopher Simpson (1605-1669)
A Compendium of Practical Music

This third edition was first published in 1678.

Reprinted 2007 by Travis & Emery Music Bookshop
17 Cecil Court, London, WC2N 4EZ, England.
Tel. (+44) 20 7240 2129.

Hardback: ISBN: 1-904331-26-2.   ISBN13: 978-1904331-26
Paperback: ISBN: 1-904331-27-0.   ISBN13: 978-1904331-27

W. Faithorne del. et sculp.

Christophori Simpson Effigies.

A COMPENDIUM
OF
Practical Musick
IN FIVE PARTS.

Teaching, by a New, and easie Method,

1. The Rudiments of Song.
2. The Principles of Composition.
3. The Use of Discords.
4. The Form of Figurate Descant.
5. The Contrivance of Canon.

Together with
LESSONS for VIOLS, &c.

The Third Editio.

By *CHRISTOPHER SIMPSON.*

PSAL. cxlix.
Cantate Domino Canticum novum.
Laus ejus in Ecclesia Sanctorum.

LONDON,
Printed by *M.C.* for *Henry Brome,* at the *Gun* near the West-end of St. *Pauls.*
M DC LXXVIII.

TO THE
READER.

THE Esteem I ever had for Mr. *Simpson*'s Perſon, and Morals, has not engag'd me in any ſort of Partiality to his Works: but I am yet glad of any occaſion wherein I may fairly ſpeak a manifeſt Truth to his Advantage; and at the ſame time, do a Juſtice to the Dead, and a Service to the Living.

This *Compendium* of his, I look upon as the Cleareſt, the moſt Uſeful, and Regular Method of Introduction to Muſick that is yet Extant. And herein I do but joyn in a Teſtimony with greater Judges. This is enough ſaid on the Behalf of a Book that carries in it ſelf its own Recommendation.

Roger L'Eſtrange.

Licensed. *March* 15,
1678.
Roger L'Estrange.

THE
PREFACE.

I *Have always been of opinion, that if a man had made any discovery, by which an Art or Science might be learnt, with less expence of Time and Travel, he was obliged in common duty, to communicate the Knowledge thereof to others. This is the chief (if not only) motive which hath begot this little Treatise.*

And though I know a man can scarcely write upon any Subject of this nature, but the substance will be the same in effect which hath been taught before; yet thus much I may affirm; that the Method is new; and (as I hope) both plain and easie: and some things also, are explicated, which I have not seen mentioned in any former Author.

I must acknowledge, I have taken some Parcels out of a Book I formerly publish'd, to make up this Compendium: *But I hope it is no Theft to make use of ones own; This being intended for such as have no occasion to use the Other. Also, the First Part of this Book was Printed by it self, upon a particular occasion: but*

with

The Preface.

with intention and intimation of adding the other Parts thereto, so soon as they were ready for the Press, and the Press for them.

Every man is pleased with his own Conceptions: but no man can deliver that which shall please all men. Some perhaps will be dissatisfied with my Method, in teaching the Principles of Composition, *the* Use of Discords, *and* Figurate Descant, *in three distinct discourses, which others commonly teach together, promiscuously: But, I am clearly of opinion, that the* Principles of Composition *are best established in plain* Counterpoint; *And the* Use *of* Discords *must be known, before* Figurate Descant *can be formed.*

Others may object, that I fill up several Pages with things superfluous; as namely, my Discourse of Greater *and* Lesser Semitones; *and my shewing that all the* Concords, *and other* Intervals *of* Musick, *arise from the division of a* Line *or* String *into equal Parts; which are not the concernments of* Practical Musick. *'Tis granted: But my demonstrations of them are Practical; and, though some do not regard such things, yet others (I doubt not) will be both satisfied and delighted with the knowledge of them.*

If this which I now exhibit shall any way promote or facilitate the Art of Musick *(of which I profess my self a zealous* Lover *) I have obtained the Scope of my desires, and the end of my endeavours. Or, if any man else, by my*
Example

The Preface.

Example, shall endeavour to render it yet more easie, which I heartily wish, I shall be glad that I gave some occasion thereof. There is no danger of bringing Musick into contempt upon that accompt: The better it is known and understood, the more it will be valued and esteemed: and those that are most Skilful, may still find new occasions (if they please) to improve their knowledge by it.

I will not detain you too long in my Preface; *only, let me desire you,* First, *to read over the whole Discourse, that you may know the designment of it.* Next, *when you begin where you have occasion for instruction, (if you desire to be instructed by it) that you make your self perfect in* That *particular (and so, of each other) before you proceed to the next following : By which means your progress in it will be, both more sure, and more speedy.* Lastly, *that you receive it with the like Candor and Integrity with which it is offered to you, by*

Your Friend and Servant

C. S.

To

To his much Honoured
and very precious Friend

Mr. CHRISTOPHER SIMPSON.

SIR,

HAving perus'd your Excellent *Compendium of Musick* (so far as my time and your pressing occasion could permit) I confess it my greatest Concern to thank you for the Product of so ingenious a Work as tends to the improvement of the whole frame; (I mean as to the least and most knowing Capacities in the Rudiments of that Science.) To speak in a word; The Subject, Matter, Method, the Platform and rational Materials wherewith you raise and beautifie this Piece, are such as will erect a lasting Monument to the Author, and oblige the World as much to serve him, as he that is,

Sir,

Your most Affectionate

Friend and Servant

JOHN JENKINS.

To all Lovers of Harmony.

PRincess of *Order*, whose eternal Arms
　　Puts *Chaos* into *Concord*, by whose charms
The *Cherubims* in *Anthems* clear and even
Create a *Consort* for the *King of Heaven*,
Inspire me with thy *Magick*, that my *Numbers*
May rock the *never-sleeping Soul* in slumbers:
Tune up my *LYRE*, that when I *sing* thy merits
My *subdivided Notes* may sprinkle spirits
Into my *Auditory*, whilst their fears
Suggest their *Souls* are sallying through their Ears.
What *Tropes* and *Figures* can thy glory reach,
That art thy self the *splendor* of all *speech*!
Mysterious Musick! He that doth thee *right*
Must shew thy *Excellence* by thine own *Light*:
Thy *Purity* must *teach* us how *to prayse*;
As men seek out the *Sun* with his own *rayes*.
What *Creature* that hath *being*, *life* or *sense*,
But wears the *Badges* of thine *influence*?
Musick is *Harmony*, whose copious bounds
Is not confined only unto *Sounds*,
'Tis the eyes *object*, for (without Extortion)
It comprehends all things that have *proportion*.
Musick *is Concord*, and doth *hold* allusion
With every thing that doth *oppose* confusion.
In comely *Architecture* it may be
Known by the Name of *Uniformity*;
Where *Pyramids* to *Pyramids* relate,
And the whole *Fabrick* doth configurate;
In perfectly *proportion'd* Creatures we
Accept it by the title *SYMMETRIE*:
When many men for some *design* convent,
And all *concentre*, it is call'd *CONSENT*:
Where mutual hearts in *Sympathy* do move,
Some few *embrace* it by the name of *LOVE*:
　　　　　　　　　　　　　　　　　But

But where the *Soul* and *Body* do agree
To *serve* their *God*, it is *DIVINITIE*:
In all *Melodious Compositions* we
Declare and know it to be *SYMPHONIE*:
Where all the Parts in Complication roll,
And every one contributes to the whole.
He that can Sett and Humour Notes aright,
Will move the Soul to Sorrow, to Delight,
To Courage, Courtesie, to Consolation,
To Love, to Gravity, to Contemplation :
It hath been known (by its *magnetick motion*)
To *raise Repentance,* and *advance Devotion.*
It *works* on all the *Faculties,* and why?
The very *Soul* it self is *Harmony.*
Musick ! it is the *breath* of *Second Birth,*
The *Saints Imployment,* and the *Angels mirth* ;
The *Rhetorick* of *Seraphims* ; a *Gem*
In the *Kings Crown* of *new Jerusalem :*
They *sing continually ,* the Exposition
Must needs infer, there is *no Intermission.*
I hear, some men hate Musick , Let them show
In holy Writ *what else the Angels do :*
Then those that do despise such sacred Mirth
Are neither fit for Heaven nor for Earth.

The

Contents of the first Part.

§ 1. Of the Scale of Musick. Pag. 1.
§ 2. Of naming the Degrees of Sound. 3.
§ 3. Concerning ♭ flat and ♯ sharp. 5.
§ 4. Of Tuning the Degrees of Sound. 6.
§ 5. Of Notes, their Names and Characters. 10.
§ 6. Of the Antient Moods, or Measures of Notes. 11.
§ 7. Of keeping Time. 14.
§ 8. Of Driving a Note. 19.
§ 9. Cooncerning odd Rests. 21.
§ 10. Of Tripla-Time. 23.
§ 11. Of Diminution. 27.

Contents of the second Part.

§ 1. Of Counterpoint. 29.
§ 2. Of Intervals. 30.
§ 3. Of Concords. 31.
§ 4. Passage of the Concords. 32.
§ 5. Concerning the Key or Tone. 34.
§ 6. Of the Closes or Cadences belonging to the Key. 36.
§ 7. How to frame a Bass. 37.
§ 8. How to joyn a Treble to the Bass. 38.
§ 9. Composition of three Parts. 42.
§ 10. Composition of four Parts. 44.
§ 11. How a 5th. and a 6th. may stand together in Counterpoint. 47.

§ 12.

The Contents.

§ 12. *Composition in a sharp Key.* 48.
§ 13. *Of Transition or Breaking a Note.* 51.
§ 14. *Composition of 5, 6, and 7 Parts.* 53.
§ 15. *Of two Basses, and Composition of Eight Parts.* 57.

Contents of the third Part.

§ 1. *Concerning Discords.* 61.
§ 2. *How Discords are admitted into Musick.* 62.
§ 3. *Of Syncopation.* 63.
§ 4. *Passage of Discords.* 66.
§ 5. *Of Discords Note against Note.* 67.
§ 6. *Of Discords in double Transition.* 69.
§ 7. *Of Relation Inharmonical.* 71.
§ 8. *Of the three Scales of Musick.* 76.
§ 9. *Of Greater and Lesser Semitones.* 79.
§ 10. *Where these Greater and Lesser Semitones arise in the Scale of Musick.* 83.

Contents of the fourth Part.

§ 1. *What is meant by Figurate Descant.* 85.
§ 2. *Of the* Greek *Moods and* Latin *Tones.* 86.
§ 3. *Of Figurate Musick in general.* 89.
§ 4. *How to set a Bass to a Treble.* 90.
§ 5. *How Parts pass through one another.* 93.
§ 6. *Concerning the Consecution of Perfects of the same kind; and of other Disallowances in Composition.* 94.
§ 7. *Concerning the Consecution of 4ths. and 5ths.* 99.

§ 8.

The Contents.

§ 8. *Confecution of 3ds. and 6ths.*   102.
§ 9. *Of Fuga or Fuge.*   104.
§ 10. *Of* Arſin & Theſin.   106.
§ 11. *Of Double Fuges.*   108.
§ 12. *How to form a Fuge.*   110.
§ 13. *Of Muſick Compoſed for Voices.*   112.
§ 14. *Of accommodating Notes to Words.* 114.
§ 15. *Of Muſick deſign'd for Inſtruments.* 115.

Contents of the fifth Part.

§ 1. *Concerning Canon.*   119.
§ 2. *Canon of two Parts.*   120.
§ 3. *Canon of three Parts.*   124.
§ 4. *Of Canon in Uniſon.*   126.
§ 5. *Of Syncopated or Driving Canon.*   127.
§ 6. *Of Canon a Note Higher or Lower.* 133.
§ 7. *Of Canon Riſing and Falling a Note.* 135.
§ 8. *Of Retrograde Canon, or Canon* Recte & Retro.   Ibid.
§ 9. *Of Double Deſcant.*   138.
§ 10. *Of Canon to a Plain-ſong propoſed.* 140.
§ 11. *Of Catch or Round.*   143.

PROEM.

The *Object* of this *Science is Sound*; and That *Sound is* two ways to be *considered:* as *First*, whether *Grave* or *Acute*. Secondly, whether *Long* or *Short*, as to duration of *Time*. The *first* of these *is* regulated by the *Scale of Musick*: The *Later*, by certain *Notes*, *Marks*, or *Signs* invented for that purpose. And these *Two* (called Tune and Time) *are the subject of the first part of this Treatise*, and the Foundation upon which the other Parts are raised. The second Part shews, how *Grave* and *Acute Sounds* are joyned together in *Musical Concordance.* The third Part brings *Discords* into *Harmony*: And out of these two (viz. *Concords* and *Discords*) *is* formed the fourth Part, named *Figurate Descant*. The fifth Part leads *Figurate Descant* into *Canon*; which *is* the *Culmen*, or highest degree of *Musical Composition*.

A COMPENDIUM
OF
PRACTICAL MUSICK.

THE FIRST PART.
Teaching the Rudiments of Song.

§ 1. *Of the Scale of Musick.*

THE end and office of the *Scale of Musick* is to shew the Degrees by which a Voice Natural or Artificial may either ascend or descend. These Degrees are numbred by *Sevens*. To speak of the mystery of that number, were to deviate from the business in hand. Let it suffice that Musick may be taught by any names of things, so the number of *Seven* be observed in Ascending or Descending by degrees.

Our *Common Scale*, to mark or distinguish those Seven Degrees, makes use of the same Seven Letters which in the Kalender denote the Seven Days of the Week; *viz.* A, B, C, D, E, F, G. after which, follow A, B, C, &c. over again, so often repeated

B as

A Compendium of Musick.

as the Compass of Musick doth require. The Order of those Letters is such as you see in the adjoyned *Scale*; to wit, in Ascending we reckon them forward; in Descending, backward. Where note, that every eight letter, together with its degree of *Sound* (whether you reckon upward or downward) is still the like, as well in nature as denomination.

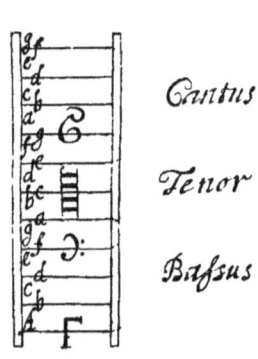

Together with these Letters, the *Scale* consists of Lines and Spaces, each Line and each Space being a several Degree, as you may perceive by the Letters standing in them.

Those Letters are called *Cliffs*, *Claves*, or *Keys*, because they open to us the meaning of every Song.

On the lowest line is commonly placed this *Greek* letter Γ, which *Guido Aretinus*, who reduced the *Greek Scale* into this form, did place at the bottom, to signifie from whence he did derive it; and from that Letter the *Scale* took the name of *Gamma*, or *Gam-ut*.

On the middle of the *Scale*, you see three of those Letters in different Characters, of which some one is set at the beginning of every Song. The lowest of them is the *F Cliff*, marked thus 𝄢 which is peculiar to the *Bass*. The highest is a *G Cliff* made thus 𝄞 and signifies the *Treble* or highest part. Betwixt these two, stands the *C Cliff*, marked thus 𝄡 which is a Fifth below the *G Cliff*, and a Fifth also above the *F Cliff*, as you may observe by compting the degrees in the *Scale*, reckoning both the terms inclu-

Rudiments of Song. 3

inclusively. This *Cliff*, standing in the middle, serves for all Inner parts.

When we see any one of these, we know thereby what part it is, and also what Letters belong to each Line and Space, which, though (for brevity) not set down at large, are, notwithstanding supposed to be in those five Lines and Spaces, in such order and manner as they stand in the Scale it self.

Example.

Bass.   Inner part.   Treble.

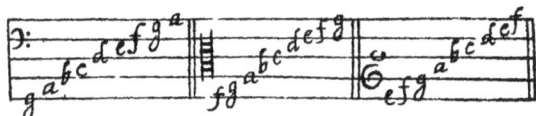

§ 2. *Of naming the Degrees of Sound.*

BEfore we come to the Tuning of these Degrees, you may observe, that a voice doth express a Sound best, when it pronounceth some word or syllable with it. For this cause, as also for order and distinction sake, six Syllables were used in former times, viz. *Ut*, *Re*, *Mi*, *Fa*, *Sol*, *La*, which being joyned with the Seven Letters, their *Scale* was set down in this manner, as follows.

Four

e la
d la sol ─────
c sol fa
b fa ✵ *mi* ─────
a la mi re
g sol re ut 𝄞 ──
f fa ut
e la mi ─────
d la sol re
c sol fa ut 𝄡 ──
b fa ✵ *mi*
a la mi re ─────
g sol re ut
F fa ut 𝄢 ──
E la mi
D sol re ─────
C fa ut
B mi ─────
A re
Γ ut ─────

Four of these, to wit, *Mi, Fa, Sol, La,* (taken in their significancy) are necessary assistants to the right Tuning of the Degrees of Sound, as will presently appear. The other two, *Ut* and *Re*, are superfluous, and therefore laid aside by most Modern Teachers.

We will therefore make use only of *Mi, Fa, Sol, La,* and apply them to the Seven Letters, which stand for the Degrees of *Sound.* In order to which, we must first find out where *Mi* is to be placed; which being known, the places of the other three are known by consequence, for *Mi* hath always *Fa, Sol, La,* both above it and under it, in such order and manner as you see them set in the Margin. I will therefore only give you a Rule for placing of *Mi*, and the work is done.

la
sol
fa
mi
la
sol
fa

A Rule for placing of Mi.

THe first and most natural place for *Mi* is in *B.*
But if you find in that line or space which belongs to *B,* such a little mark or letter as this [♭] which is called a ♭ *flat*, and excludes *Mi* wheresoever it comes, then is *Mi* to be placed in *E,* which is its second natural place. If *E* have also a ♭ *flat* in it, then of necessity, you must place your *Mi* in *A.*

Rudiments of Song.

I have seen Songs with a ♭ *flat* standing in *A*, in *B*, and in *E*, all at once, by which means *Mi* has been extruded from all its three places: but such Songs are irregular, (as to that which we call the *sol-fa-ing* of a Song) being designed for Instruments rather than for Voices: However, if any such Song should be proposed to you, place your *Mi* in *D*, with *fa*, *sol*, *la*, above it and under it, as formerly delivered.

§ 3. *Concerning* ♭ flat, *and* ♯ sharp.

AS for the ♭ *flat* we last mentioned, take notice, that when it is set at the beginning of a Song, it causes all the Notes standing in that Line or Space, to be called *Fa*, throughout the whole Song. In any other place, it serves only for that particular Note before which it is placed. Mark also, (and bear it well in mind) that wheresoever you sing *Fa*, that *Fa* is but the distance of a *Semitone* or *Half-Note* from the Sound of that degree which is next under it; which *Semitone*, together with its *Fa*, must of necessity come twice in every *Octave*; the reason whereof is, that the two principal Concords in Musick (which are a *Fifth* and an *Eighth*) would, without that abatement, be thrust out of their proper places. But this you will better understand hereafter.

There is yet another Mark in Musick, necessary to be known in order to the right Tuning of a Song, which is this ♯ called a *sharp*. This *sharp* is of a contrary nature to the ♭ *flat*, for, whereas that ♭ takes away a *Semitone* from the sound of the Note before which it is set, to make it more *grave* or *flat*; This ♯ doth add a *Semitone* to his Note to make it more *acute* or *sharp*.

6   *A Compendium of Musick.*

If it be set at the beginning of a Song, it makes all the Notes standing in that Line or Space, to be *sharp*; that is, half a Tone higher, throughout the whole Song or Lesson, without changing their Name. In any other place, it serves only for that particular Note to which it is applyed.

§ 4. *Of Tuning the Degrees of Sound.*

Tuning is no way to be taught but by Tuning, and therefore you must procure some who know how to Tune these Degrees (which every one doth that hath but the least Skill in Musick) to Sing them over with you, until you can tune them by your self.

If you have been accustomed to any Instrument that hath *Frets*, as *Viol, Lute, Theorbo,* &c. you may by help thereof (instead of an assisting voice) guide or lead your own voice to the perfect Tuning of them. For every Degree is that distance of Sound which is found upon any fretted Instrument from the open String to the second Fret, or from any one Fret, to the next but one to it; except that Sound to which we apply *fa*; for *fa,* is always but the distance of one Fret from the Sound of the Degree next under it.

We will take the Bass-Viol for Example, in the Common old Tuning, and in the way of *Tableture,* where six Lines stand for the six Strings of the *Viol,* (the highest for the highest or *Treble* String, and so the rest in order) and Letters are set for the Frets, (though in a different way from the Scale of Musick) to wit [*a*] for the *open string,* [*b*] for the first *fret,* [*c*] for the *second,* and so the rest in order; each *fret* making the Distance or Interval of a *Semitone,* or *Half-Note.*

Example.

Rudiments of Song.

Example.

```
        Tuning.              Frets.
    1  a_____ a b  r  d  e  f  g  h
    2  f  a     ‖a b |r |d |e |f |g |h‖
 S  3     f  a  ‖a b |r |d |e |f |g |h‖
 t  4        e  a ‖a b |r |d |e |f |g |h‖
 r  5           f a‖a b |r |d |e |f |g |h‖
 i  6              f‖a b |r |d |e |f |g |h‖
 n                   1  2  3  4  5  6  7
 g
 s
```

Our business now, is, to make these Letters teach you to rise and fall by degrees with your Voice, in case you have no other assistant. We will make use of the *middle Cliff*, and take the Compass of an *Octave*, (because an *Octave* includes the chief concernments of Musick) and so place the Letters of *Tableture*, and the degrees of Sound one over the other, that you may compare them, both with your Eye and your Ear.

B 4 Example.

8. *A Compendium of Musick.*

Example.

Mi in B.

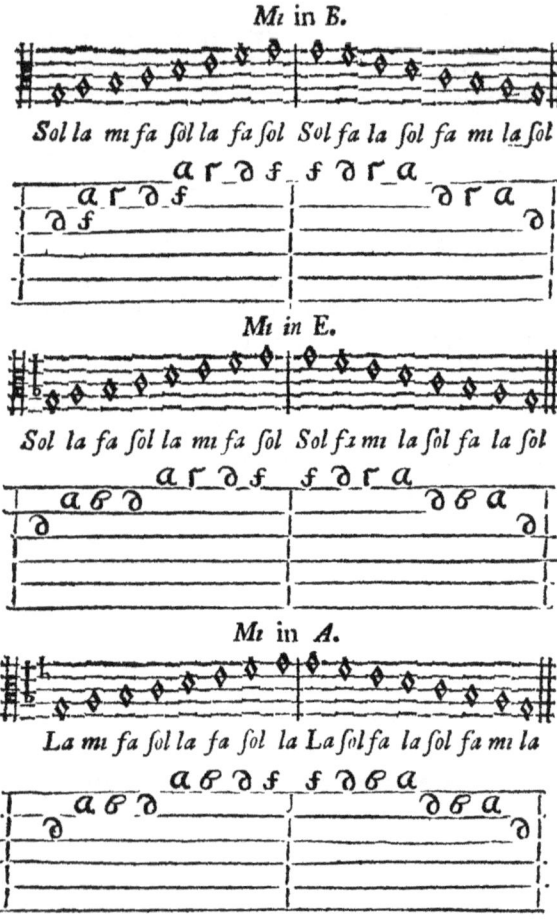

Sol la mi fa sol la fa sol Sol fa la sol fa mi la sol

Mi in E.

Sol la fa sol la mi fa sol Sol fa mi la sol fa la sol

Mi in A.

La mi fa sol la fa sol la La sol fa la sol fa mi la

And here you may observe what an advantage these four Syllables do afford us towards the right Tuning

Rudiments of Song. 9

Tuning of the Degrees, for, as *Mi* directs apt and fitting places for *fa, sol,* and *la,* to stand in due order both above and under it, So *fa* doth shew us where we are to place the *Semitone* or *Half-Note*; which (as I said) must have two places in each *Octave*, that the Degrees may meet the two Concords in their proper places.

Now, as you have seen the three places of *Mi* in the *C Cliff,* the like is to be understood of the other two *Cliffs*, according to the Examples following.

When you have brought your Voice to rise and fall by Degrees in manner aforesaid, I would then have you exercise it to ascend and descend by leaps, to all the distances in an *Octave*, both *flat* and *sharp* in manner as follows:

Example.

10   *A Compendium of Musick.*

Example.

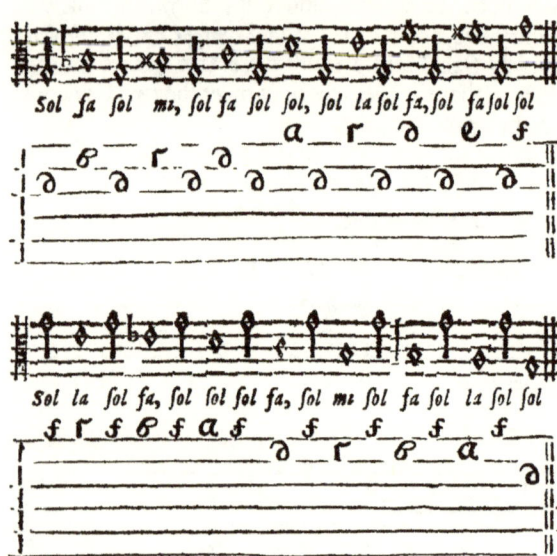

Having spoken of Naming and Tuning of sounds, it now comes in order that we treat of their length or quantity, according to measure of *Time*; which is the second concernment or consideration of a sound.

§ 5. *Of Notes, their Names and Characters.*

THe first two notes in use, were *Nota Longa & Nota Brevis*, (our *Long* and *Breve*) in order to a long and short syllable. Only they doubled or trebled their *Longa*, and called it *Larga*, or *Maxima Nota*, which is our *Large*.

When Musick grew to more perfection, they added two Notes more, under the Names of *semi brevis*
and

Rudiments of Song.

and *Minima Nota*; (our *Semibreve* and *Minim*) which later was then their shortest Note.

To these, later times have added Note upon Note, till at last we are come to *Demisemiquaver*; which is the shortest or swiftest Note that we have now in practice. The Characters and Names of which Notes are these that follow,

The strokes or marks which you see set after them, are called *Pauses* or *Rests*; (that is, a cessation or intermission of sound) and are of the same length or quantity (as to measure of time) with the Notes which stand before them, and are likewise called by the same names, as *Long Rest*, *Breve Rest*, *Semibreve Rest*, &c.

And now from the Names and Characters of Notes, we will proceed to their measures, quantities, and proportions.

§ 6. *Of the Antient Moods or Measures of Notes.*

IN former times they had four *Moods*, or *Modes* of measuring Notes. The first they called *Perfect of the More*, (*Time* and *Prolation* being implyed) in which a *Large* contained three *Longs*, a *Long* three *Breves*, a *Breve* three *Semibreves*, and a *Semibreve* three *Minims*: so it is set down in later Authors, though

I make a doubt whether *Semibreves* and *Minims* (at least *Minims*) were ever used in this *Mood*. Its sign was this, ⊙ 3.

The second *Mood* had the name of *Perfect of the Less*. In this, a *Large* contained two *Longs*, a *Long* two *Breves*, a *Breve* three *Semibreves*, and a *Semibreve* two *Minims*. The *Time* or *Measure-Note* in this *Mood* was the *Breve*, the sign or mark of the *Mood* was this, O 3.

The third *Mood* was named *Imperfect of the More*. In which a *Large* contained two *Longs*, a *Long* two *Breves*, a *Breve* two *Semibreves*, and a *Semibreve* (which was the *Time-Note* in this *Mood*) contained three *Minims*. Its mark or sign was this, C 3.

The measure of these three *Moods* was *Tripla*, of which more hereafter. To tell you their distinction of *Mood*, *Time*, and *Prolation*, were to little purpose; the *Moods* themselves wherein they were concerned, being now worn out of use.

The fourth *Mood* they named *Imperfect of the Less*, which we now call the *Common Mood*, the other three being laid aside as useless. The sign of this *Mood* is a *Semicircle*, thus, C, sometimes with a dash or stroke through it, thus, ₵. And this is commonly set at the beginning of Songs and Lessons. Though there be no sign, you may suppose this *Mood*, because the rest are grown strangers to us. You may sometimes see this Figure 3 set at the beginning of a Song or Lesson, of which I shall speak hereafter.

In this last or common *Mood*, two *Longs* make one *Large*, two *Breves* a *Long*, two *Semibreves* a *Breve*, &c. In which order they proceed to the last or shortest Note: So that a *Large* contains two *Longs*, four *Breves*, eight *Semibreves*, sixteen *Minims*, thirty two *Crochets*, sixty four *Quavers*, &c. which (for your

Rudiments of Song.

your better underſtanding) is preſented to your view in the following Scheme.

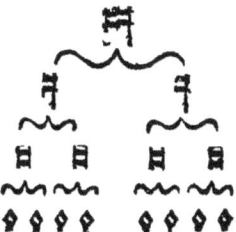

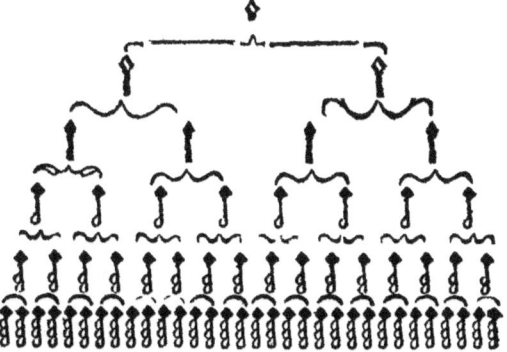

Where note, that the *Large* and *Long* are now of little uſe, being too long for any Voice or Inſtrument (the Organ excepted) to hold out to their full length. But their *Reſts* are ſtill in frequent uſe, eſpecially in grave Muſick, and Songs of many Parts.

You will ſay, If thoſe Notes you named be too long for the Voice to hold out, to what purpoſe were they uſed formerly? To which I anſwer, they were uſed in *Tripla Time*, and in a quick Meaſure; quicker (perhaps) than we now make our *Semibreve* and *Minim*. For, as After-times added new Notes, ſo they ('ſtill) put back the former into ſomething a ſlower Meaſure.

§ 7. *Of*

§ 7. *Of keeping* Time.

Our next business is, to consider how (in such a diversity of long and short Notes) we come to give every particular Note its due Measure, without making it either longer or shorter than it ought to be. To effect this, we use a constant motion of the Hand. Or if the Hand be otherwise employed, we use the Foot. If that be also ingaged, the Imagination (to which these are but assistant) is able of it self to perform that Office. But in this place we must have recourse to the motion of of the Hand.

This motion of the Hand is *Down* and *Up*, successively and equally divided. Every *Down* and *Up* being called a *Time* or *Measure*. And by this we measure the length of a *Semibreve*; which is therefore called the *Measure-Note*, or *Time-Note*. And therefore, look how many of the shorter Notes go to a *Semibreve*, (as you did see in the *Scheme*) so many do also go to every *Time* or *Measure*. Upon which accompt, two *Minims* make a *Time*, one down, the other up; Four *Crochets* a *Time*, two down, and two up. Again, Eight *Quavers* a *Time*, four down, and four up. And so you may compute the rest.

But you may say, I have told you that a *Semibreve* is the length of a *Time*, and a *Time* the length of a *Semibreve*, and still you are ignorant what that length is.

To which I answer, (in case you have none to guide your Hand at the first measuring of Notes) I would have you pronounce these words [*One, Two, Three, Four*] in an equal length, as you would (leisurely) read them: Then fancy those four words to be four *Crochets*, which make up the quantity

Rudiments of Song. 15

tity or length of a *Semebreve*, and consequently of a *Time* or *Measure*: In which, let these two words [*One, Two*] be pronounced with the Hand Down; and [*Three, Four*] with it Up. In the continuation of this motion you will be able to Measure and compute all your other Notes. Some speak of having recourse to the motion of a lively pulse for the measure of *Crochets*; or to the little Minutes of a steddy going Watch for *Quavers*, by which to compute the length of other Notes, but this which I have delivered, will (I think) be most useful to you.

It is now fit that I set you some easie and short Lesson or Song, to exercise your Hand in keeping *Time*; to which purpose this which follows shall serve in the first place; with *Mi* in *B*, according to what hath been delivered: where observe, that when you see a Prick or Point like this [·] set after any Note, That Note must have half so much as its value comes to, added to it: That is if it be a *Semibreve*, that *Semibreve*, with its Prick, must be holden out the length of three *Minims*: If it stand after a *Minim*, that *Minim* and the Prick must be made the length of three *Crochets*: but still to be Sung or Played as one entire Note. And so you may conceive of a Prick after any other Note.

Here you have every Time or Measure distinguished by strokes crossing the Lines, which strokes (together with the Spaces betwixt them) are called *Bars*. In the third *Bar* you have a *Minum* with a Prick after it; which *Minum* and Prick must be made the length of three *Crochets*. In the Eight *Bar* you have a *Minum Rest* which you must (silently) measure, as two *Crochets*, according to the two Figures you see under it

The second Staff or Stanza is the same as the first; only it is broken into *Crochets*, (four of which make a Time) by which you may exactly measure the Notes which stand above them, according to our proposed Method.

When you can sing the former Example in exact Time, you may try this next, which hath *Mi* in E.

Rudiments of Song. 17

In the eight Bar of this Example you have a *Minim Rest* and a *Crochet Rest* standing both together, which you may reckon as three *Crochet Rests*, according to the Figures which stand under them.

This mark √ which you see at the end of the five Lines, is set to direct us where the first Note of the next five Lines doth stand, and is therefore called a *Directer*.

We will now proceed to quicker Notes, in which, we must turn our dividing *Crochets* into *Quavers*, Four whereof must be Sung with the Hand *down*, and four with it *up*.

Your Example shall be set with a *G Cliff*, and *Mi* in *A*, that you may be ready in naming your Notes, in any of the *Cliffs*.

C   Example.

Example.

Here you have a *Prickt-Crochet* (or *Crochet* with a Prick after it) divided into three *Quavers*, in several places of this Example, expressed by the *Quavers* in the under Staff: which *Quavers* I would have you to sing or play often over, that they may Teach you the true length of your *Prickt-Crochet*, which is of very much concernment for Singing or Playing exactly in Time.

When you see an *Arch* or *Stroke* drawn over or under two, three, or more Notes, like those in the lower

Rudiments of Song.

lower Staff of the late Example, it signifies in Vocal Musick, so many Notes to be Sung to one Syllable; (as Ligatures did in former times) in Musick made for Viols or Violins, it signifies so many Notes to be played with one motion of the Bow.

Two strokes through the Lines signifie the end of a Strain. If they have Pricks on each side thus, the Strain is to be repeated.

This Mark ℒ signifies a Repetition from that place only where it is set, and is called a *Repeat*.

This Mark or Arch ⌒ is commonly set at the end of a Song or Lesson, to signifie the Close or Conclusion. It is also set, sometimes, over certain particular Notes in the middle of Songs, when (for humor) we are to insist or stay a little upon the said Notes; and thereupon it is called a *Stay*, or *Hold*.

§ 8. *Of driving a Note.*

Syncope, or Driving a Note, is, when after some shorter Note which begins the Measure or Half-measure, there immediately follow two, three, or more Notes of a greater quantity, before you meet with another short Note (like that which began the driving) to make the number even, as when an odd *Crochet* comes before two, three, or more *Minims*; or an odd *Quaver* before two, three, or more *Crochets*.

To facilitate this, divide always the Greater Note into two of the Lesser, that is, if they be *Minims*, divide them into two *Crochets* a piece; if *Crochets*, into two *Quavers*.

A Compendium of Musick.

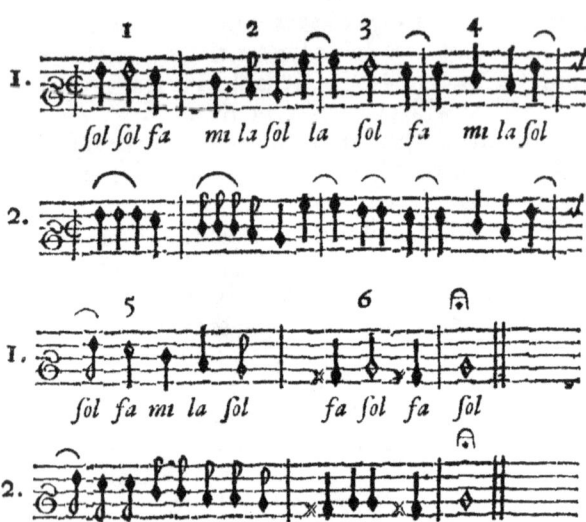

In this Example, the first Note is a *Crochet*, which *drives* through the *Minim* in *D*, and the Measure is made even by the next *Crochet* in *C*.

The second *Barr* begins with a *Prickt-Crochet*, which is divided into three *Quavers*, in the lower Staff, as formerly shewed. In the same *Bar* the *Crochet* in *G*, is *driven* through three *Minims*, *viz.* those in *E*, *D*, *C*, and the number is made even by the *Crochet* in *B*, which answers to that *Crochet* which begun the *driving*. The fifth *Bar* begins with a *Quaver*, which is driven through the three *Crochets*, standing in *C*, *B*, *A*, and is made even by the *Quaver* in *G*, which answers to it, and fills up the measure. All which is made easie by dividing them into such lesser Notes as you see in the lower Staff.

§ 9. *Con-*

§ 9. *Concerning odd* Rests.

ODd *Rests* we call those which take up only some part or parcel of a *Semibreves* Time or Measure, and have always reference to some odd Note; for, by these two *Odds* the Measure is made even.

Their most usual place is the Beginning or Middle of the Time, yet somtimes they are set in the latter part of it, as it were, to fill up the Measure.

If you see a short *Rest* stand before one that is longer, you may conclude that the short *Rest* is set there in reference to some odd Note which went before: For there is no such thing as *driving* a shorter *Rest* through a longer, like that which we shewed in Notes.

When two *Minim Rests* stand together (in common Time) you may suppose that the first of them belongs to the foregoing Time, and the second to the Time following; otherwise they would have been made one entire *Semibreve-Rest*.

When we have a *Minim-Rest* with a *Crochet-Rest* after it, we commonly count them as three *Crochet-Rests*. In like manner we reckon a *Crochet* and a *Quaver-Rest* as three *Quaver-Rests*, and a *Quaver* and *Semiquaver* as three *Semiquaver-Rests*.

Concerning the *Minim* and *Crochet-Rest*, I need say no more, supposing you are already well enough informed in their measure, by what has been delivered: The chief difficulty is in the other two, to wit, the *Quaver* and the *Semiquaver-Rests*, which, indeed, are most concern'd in Instrumental Musick.

Your best way to deal with these at first, is to play them, as you would do Notes of the same quantity: placing those supposed or feigned Notes, in such places as you think most convenient. I will give you one Example, which being well consider'd and practis'd will do the business.

22 *A Compendium of Musick*

Practice this Example, first according to the second or lower Staff. And when you have made that perfect, leave out the Notes which have Crosses over them (together with the Bows which did express them) and then it will be the same as the first Staff. By this means you will get a Habit of making these short *Rests* in their due measure.

The Notes you see with one dash or stroke through their Tails, are *Quavers*. Those with two strokes are *Semiquavers*. When they have three or four strokes, they are *Demisemiquavers*.

§ 10. *Of*

§ 10. *Of* Tripla Time.

WHen you see this Figure [3] set at the beginning of a Song or Lesson, it signifies that the Time or Measure must be compted by *Threes*, as we formerly did it by *Fours*.

Somtimes the *Tripla* consists of three *Semibreves* to a Measure, each *Semibreve* being shorter than a *Minim* in Common Time.

The Measure of this *Tripla* is like the Mood we formerly mentioned, called *Perfect of the Less*; in which, three *Semibreves* went to a *Measure*.

The more *common Tripla*, is three *Minims* to a Measure, each *Minim* about the length of a *Crochet* in Common time, and this *Tripla* is the same as the Mood *Imperfect of the More*, as to measure of *Time*; only we compt but two *Minims* to a *Semibreve*, which in that Mood contained three.

In those two sorts of *Tripla*, we compt or imagine these two words [*One, Two*] with the Hand *down*, and this word [*Three*] with it *up*. I will set down their Examples in the *Bass Cliff*, because hitherto we have made no use of it.

A Compendium of Musick.

Tripla of 3 Semibreves to a Measure.

When the shorter Note comes before the longer, in the same Time or Measure (as in two places of this last Example, marked with little Crosses) it is usual with some to make them both black, in this manner.

The like they do also in *Tripla*'s of Three *Minims*, when the *Minim* comes before the *Semibreve*, thus, which I suppose they do, only to shew that the short Note belongs to that which follows, not to that which went before, seeing they do not intend thereby any diminution of their value, which blacking of Notes doth properly signifie, as will be shewed hereafter.

Tripla

Rudiments of Song. 25

Tripla *of three* Minims *to a Measure*,

There are divers *Tripla's* of a shorter Measure, which by reason of their quick movement, are usually measured by compting three down, and three up, with the Hand; so that of them it may be said that two Measures make but one time. And those quick *Tripla's* are prickt somtimes with *Minims* and *Crochets*; and somtimes with black *Semibreves* instead of *Minims*; and black *Minims*, which in appearance are *Crochets*. I will set you one Example prickt both ways, that you may not be ignorant of either when they shall be laid before you.

Tripla

Tripla *of three* Crochets *to a Measure.*

Take notice that the black *Semibreves*, as also the *Minims* which stand over them, are sung or play'd as fast in these quick *Tripla's*, as *Crochets* in Common Time; and the black *Minims* or *Crochets* (call them which you pleaſe) as faſt as *Quavers*. The like conſideration may be had of the former *Tripla's*, as well of three *Semibreves* as three *Minims* to a Meaſure; for in all *Tripla's* the Notes are ſung or play'd much quicker than they are in Common Time.

Beſide theſe ſeveral ſorts of *Tripla's* before mentioned, you may ſomtimes meet with Figures ſet thus ¾ called *Sesquialtera* proportion, which ſignifies a *Tripla* Meaſure of three Notes to two ſuch like Notes of the Common Time. The like may be underſtood of 6/4 or any other proportion: which proportions, if they be of the greater inequality, (that

is

Rudiments of Song.

is, when the greater Figure doth stand above) do always signifie Diminution, of which I will speak a little in this place.

§ 11. *Of Diminution.*

Diminution (in this acceptation) is the lessening or abating somthing of the full value or quantity of Notes, a thing much used in former times when the *Tripla Moods* were in fashion. Their first sorts of Diminution were by *Note*; by *Rest*; and by *Colour*. By *Note*, as when a *Semibreve* followed a *Breve*, (in the Mood *Perfect of the Less*) That *Breve* was to be made but two *Semibreves*, which otherwise contained three. The like was observed, if a *Minim* came after a *Semibreve*, in the Mood named *Imperfect of the More*, in which a *Semibreve* contained three *Minims*.

By *Rest*; as when such *Rests* were set after like Notes.

By *Colour*, as when any of the greater Notes, which contained three of the lesser, were made black, by which they were diminished a third part of their value.

Another sign of Diminution is the Turning of the sign of the Mood backward thus ⊃ (being still in use) which requires each Note to be play'd or sung twice so quick as when it stands the usual way. Also a dash or stroke through the sign of the Mood thus ₵ is properly a sign of Diminution; though many dash it so, without any such Intention.

They had yet more signs of Diminution; as Crossing or Double-dashing the sign of the Mood; also the setting of Figures to signifie Diminution
in

in *Dupla, Tripla, Quadrupla* proportion; with other such like, which being now out of use, I will trouble you no further with them. And this is as much as I thought necessary for Tuning and Timing of Notes, which is all that belongs to the *Rudiments of Song*.

A COMPENDIUM
OF
PRACTICAL MUSICK.

THE SECOND PART,

TEACHING

The Principles of Composition.

§ 1. *Of Counterpoint.*

Efore Notes of different Meafure were in ufe, their way of Compofing was, to fet Pricks or Points one againft another, to denote the Concords; the Length or Meafure of which Points was fung according to the quantity of the Words or Syllables which were applied to them. And becaufe, in compofing our Defcant, we fet Note againft Note, as they did Point againft Point, from thence it ftill retains the name of *Counterpoint.*

In

In reference to Composition in *Counterpoint*, I must propose unto you the *Bass*, as the Groundwork or Foundation upon which all Musical Composition is to be erected: And from this *Bass* we are to measure or compute all those Distances or Intervals which are requisite for the joyning of other Parts thereto.

§ 2. *Of Intervals.*

AN *Interval* in Musick is that Distance or Difference which is betwixt any two Sounds, where the one is more Grave, the other more Acute.

In reference to *Intervals*, we are first to consider an Unison, that is, one, or the same sound, whether produced by one single Voice, or divers Voices sounding in the same Tone.

This *Unison*, as it is the first Term to any *Interval*, so may it be considered in Musick as an Unite in *Arithmetick*, or as a Point in *Geometry*, not divisible.

As sounds are more or less distant from any supposed Unison, so do they make greater or lesser *Intervals*; upon which accompt, *Intervals* may be said to be like Numbers, *Indefinite*. But Those which we are here to consider, be only such as are contained within our common Scale of Musick, which may be divided into so many Particles or Sections (only) as there be *Semitones* or Half Notes contained in the said Scale; That is to say, Twelve in every *Octave*, as may be observed in the stops of fretted Instruments, or in the Keys of a Common *Harpsecord*, or *Organ*. Their Names are these that follow.

Unison:

Principles of Composition. 31

12. Diapason.	12. Octave or 8th.
11. Semidiapason.	11. Defective 8th.
11. Sept. major.	11. Greater 7th.
10. Sept. minor.	10. Lesser 7th.
9. Hexachordon ma.	9. Greater 6th.
8. Hexachordon mi.	8. Lesser 6th.
7. Diapente.	7. Perfect 5th.
6. Semidiapente,	6. Imperfect 5th.
6. Tritone.	6. Greater 4th.
5. Diatessaron.	5. Perfect 4th.
4. Ditone.	4. Greater 3d.
3. Semiditone.	3. Lesser 3d.
2. Tone.	2. Greater 2d.
1. Semitone.	1. Lesser 2d.
Unison.	One Sound.

Where take notice, that the *Defective 8th.* and *Greater 7th.* are the same *Interval* in the Scale of Musick. The like may be said of the *Defective 5th.* and *Greater 4th.* Also you may observe, that the Particle *Semi*, in *Semidiapason, Semidiapente*, &c. doth not signifie the Half of such an *Interval*, in Musick, but only imports a deficiency, as wanting a *Semitone* of Perfection.

Out of these *Semitones* or Half Notes, arise all those Intervals or Distances which we call Concords and Discords.

§ 3. Of Concords.

Concords in Musick are these, 3*d*. 5*th*. 6*th*. 8*th*. By which I also mean their Octaves; as 10*th*, 12*th*. 13*th*. 15*th*, &c. All other Intervals, as 2*d*. 4*th*. 7*th*. and their Octaves, reckoning from the *Bass*, are *Discords*; as you see in the following Scale.

As

As you see the Concords and Discords computed here from the lowest line upward, so are they to be reckoned from any line or space wherein any Note of the *Bass* doth stand.

Again, Concords are of two sorts; *Perfect* and *Imperfect*, as you see denoted under the Scale. *Perfects* are these, 5*th.* 8*th.* with all their Octaves. *Imperfects* are a 3*d.* 6*th.* and their Octaves, as you see in the Scale.

Imperfects have yet another distinction, to wit, the *Greater* and *Lesser* 3*d.* as also the *Greater* and *Lesser* 6*th.*

§ 4. *Passage of the Concords.*

First take notice that *Perfects* of the same kind, as two 5*ths.* or two 8*ths.* rising or falling together, are not allowed in Composition, as thus,

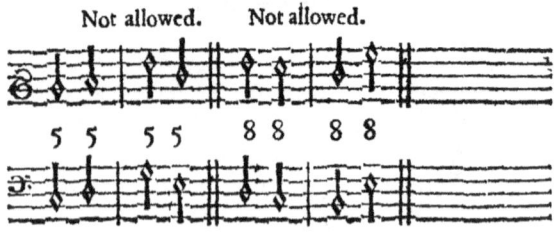

But

Principles of Composition. 33

But if the Notes do either keep still in the same line or space, or remove (upward or downward) into the Octave, two, three, or more Perfects of the same kind may in that way be allowed.

Example.

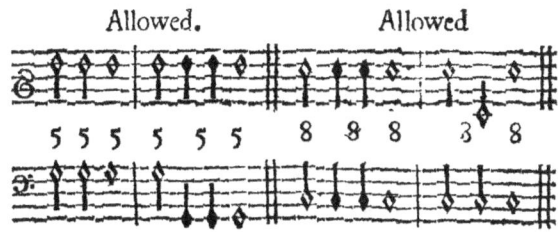

Also, in Composition of many Parts (where necessity so requires) two 5*ths.* or two 8*ths.* may be tolerated, the Parts passing in contrary Motion, thus:

Allowed in Composition of many Parts.

The passage from a 5*th.* to an 8*th.* or from an 8*th.* to a 5*th.* is (for the most part) allowable, so that the upper Part remove but one Degree.

As for 3*ds.* or 6*ths.* which are Imperfect Concords; two, three, or more of them, Ascending or Descending together, are allowable and very usual.

In fine, you have liberty to change from any one, to any other different Concord. First, when one

A Compendium of Musick.

of the Parts keeps its place. Secondly, when both the Parts remove together, some few passages excepted, as being less elegant in Composition of two or three Parts, though in more Parts more allowance may be granted to them. The passages are these that follow:

Passages not allowed in few Parts.

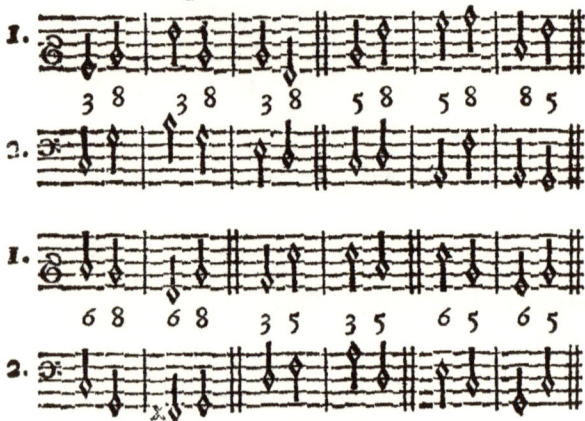

The reason why these Passages are not allowed, shall be shewed hereafter.

§ 5. *Concerning the Key or Tone.*

EVery Composition in Musick, be it long or short, is (or ought to be) designed to some one Key or Tone, in which the *Bass* doth always conclude. This Key is said to be either *Flat* or *Sharp*: not in respect of its self; but in relation to the *Flat* or *Sharp* 3*d.* which is joyned to it.

To distinguish this, you are first to consider its 5*th.* which consists always of a Lesser and a Greater 3*d.* as you see in these two Instances, the Key being in *G.*

Greater

Principles of Composition. 35

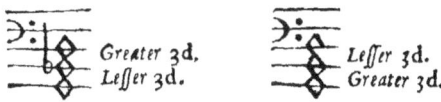

If the lesser 3 *d.* be in the lower place next to the Key, then is the Musick said to be set in a *flat* Key: But if the Greater 3 *d.* stand next to the Key, as it doth in the second Instance, then the Key is called *Sharp*.

I will shew you this *Flat* and *Sharp* 3 *d.* applyed to the Key in all the usual places of an Octave, to which may be referr'd such as are less usual, for however the Key be placed, it must always have its 5 *th.* divided according to one of these two ways; and consequently, must be either a *Flat*, or a *Sharp* Key.

Example.

36   A Compendium of Musick.

As the *Bass* is set in a *Flat* or *Sharp* Key; so must the other parts be set with *Flats* or *Sharps* in all the Octaves above it.

§ 6. *Of the Closes or Cadences belonging to the Key.*

HAving spoken of the Key or Tone; it follows, in order that we speak of the Closes or Cadences which belong unto it. And here we must have recourse to our forementioned *5th.* and its two *3ds.* for upon them depends the Aire of every Composition; they serving as Bounds or Limits which keep the Musick in a due *decorum*.

True it is, that a skilful Composer may (for variety) carry on his Musick, (sometimes) to make a middle Close or Cadence in any Key, but here we are to instruct a Beginner, and to shew him what Closes or Cadences are most proper and natural to the Key in which a Song is set.

Of these, the chief and principal is the Key it self, in which (as hath been said) the *Bass* must always conclude; and this may be used also for a middle Close near the beginning of a Song, if one think fit. The next in dignity, is the *5th.* above, and the next after that, the *3d.* In these three places middle Closes may properly be made, when the Key is *flat*.

Example.

Key Flat.

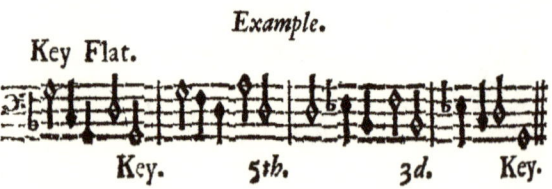

Key.   5*th*.   3*d*.   Key.

But

Principles of Composition. 37

But if the *Bass* be set in a *sharp* Key; then it is not so proper, nor easie, to make a middle Close or Cadence to end upon the *sharp* 3d. and therefore (instead thereof) we commonly make use of the 4th. or 2d. above the Key for middle Closes.

Example.

Key Sharp.

Key.   5th.   4th.   2d.   Key.

Thus you see what Closes belong to the Key, both *flat* and *sharp*: and by these two Examples set in *G*, you may know what is to be done, though the Key be removed to any other letter of the Scale.

§ 7. *How to frame a* Bass.

1. Let the Aire of your Bass be proper to the Key designed. 2. If it have middle Closes, let them be according to the late Examples. 3. The longer your *Bass* is, the more middle Closes will be required. 4. The movement of your *Bass* must be (for the most part) by leaps of a 3d. 4th. or 5th. using degrees no more than to keep it within the proper bounds and Aire of the Key. Lastly, I would have you to make choice of a *flat* Key to begin with, and avoid the setting of *sharp* Notes in the *Bass*, for some reasons which shall appear hereafter. Let this short *Bass* which follows serve for an Instance, in which there is a Close or Section at the end of the second Bar.

Example.

38 *A Compendium of Musick.*

Example.

§ 8. *How to joyn a* Treble *to the* Bass.

THe *Bass* being made, your next business is to joyn a *Treble* to it: which to effect, (after you have placed your *Treble Cliff*) you are to set a Note of the same quantity with the first Note of your *Bass*; either in a 3*d.* 5*th.* or 8*th.* above your *Bass*; for we seldom begin with a 6*th.* in *Counterpoint.*

Now, for carrying on the rest, your securest way is, to take that Concord, Note after Note, which may be had with the least remove: and that will be, either by keeping in the same place, or removing but one degree. In this manner you may proceed until you come to some Close or Section of the strain, at which you may remove by leap to what Concord you please; and then carry on the rest as before.

By this means you will be less liable to those Disallowances formerly mentioned, most of them being occasioned by leaps of the upper part.

Only let me advertise you, that we seldom use 8*ths.* in two Parts, except Beginning Notes, Ending Notes, or where the Parts move contrary: that is, one rising, the other falling.

If you set a Figure under each Note as you Prick it, to signifie what Concord it is to the *Bass*, as you see in the following Examples, it will be some ease to your Eye and Memory.

Example

Principles of Composition. 39

Example 1 beginning with a 5th.

Example 2 beginning with a 3d.

Example 3 beginning with an 8th.

Take notice that the *Bass* making a middle Close at the end of the second Bar, your *Treble* may properly remove by leap, at that place, to any other Concord, and then begin a new movement by degrees; as you see in the first Example.

I propose this movement by degrees, as the most easie, and most natural to the *Treble* part in plain *Counterpoint*: yet I do not so confine you thereto, but that you may use leaps when there shall be any occa-

40 *A Compendium of Musick.*

sion; or when your own fancy shall move you thereto: provided those Leaps be made into Imperfect Concords, as you may see by this Example.

Having told you that we seldome use 8*ths.* in two Parts, 'tis fit I give you some accompt of those in the late Examples. The first is in the third Bar of the first Example, where the *Treble* meets the *Bass* in contrary motion; therefore allowable. In the second Example are three 8*ths.* The first in the first Bar, the *Treble*-keeping its place, and therefore allowable. The second meets in contrary motion, the third keeps its place. In the third Example are two 8*ths.* the first begins the Strain, the second the Latter part thereof, in all which beginnings an 8*th.* may properly be used. Lastly, all those 8*ths.* which you see at the Conclusion of the Examples, are not only allowable, but most proper and natural.

As for those two Sharps which you see in the second Example; the first of them is disputable, as many times it happens in Musick, in which doubts the Ear is always to be Umpire. The other Sharp depends more upon a Rule, which is, that *when the Bass doth fall a* 5*th, or rise a* 4*th, that Note, from which it so rises or falls, doth commonly require the Sharp or greater* 3*d. to be joyned to it.* And being here at the conclusion, it hath a further concernment; which is, that a Binding Cadence is made of that *Greater* 3*d.* by joyning part of it to the foregoing Note, which is as frequent in Musick at

the

Principles of Composition. 41

the Close or Conclusion, as *Amen* at the end of a Prayer. Examples of it are these that follow:

This Cadence may be used by any Part which hath the *Greater 3d.* in the next Note before a Close.

There is another sort of Cadence frequent in Musick (but not at Conclusion) in which the *Greater 6th* doth lend part of its Note to the Note which went before, the *Bass* Descending a *Tone* or *Semitone*, thus:

This also is appliable by any Part, or in any Key where the *Greater 6th.* is joyned to such Notes of the *Bass*.

I would now have you frame a *Bafs* of your own, according to former Inftructions, and try how many feveral ways you can make a *Treble* to it.

When you find your felf perfect and ready therein, you may try how you can add an Inner part to your *Treble* and *Bafs*: concerning which, take thefe Inftructions.

§ 9. *Compofition of three Parts.*

First, you are to fet the Notes of this Part in Concords different from thofe of the *Treble*. 2. When the *Treble* is a 5*th*. to the *Bafs*, I would have you make ufe either of a 3*d*. or an 8*th*. for the other Part; and not to ufe a 6*th*. therewith, until I have fhewed you how, and where a 5*th*. and 6*th*. may be joyned together, of which more hereafter. 3. You are to avoid 8*ths*. in this Inner part likewife, fo much as you can with convenience. For though we ufe 5*ths*. as much as Imperfects, yet we feldome make ufe of 8*ths*. in three Parts, unlefs in fuch places as we formerly mention'd. The reafon why we avoid 8*ths* in two or three Parts, is, that Imperfect Concords afford more variety upon accompt of their *Majors* and *Minors*; befides, Imperfects do not cloy the Ear fo much as Perfects do.

We will make ufe of the former Examples, that you may perceive thereby how another Part is to be added.

Example.

Principles of Composition. 43

Example 1.

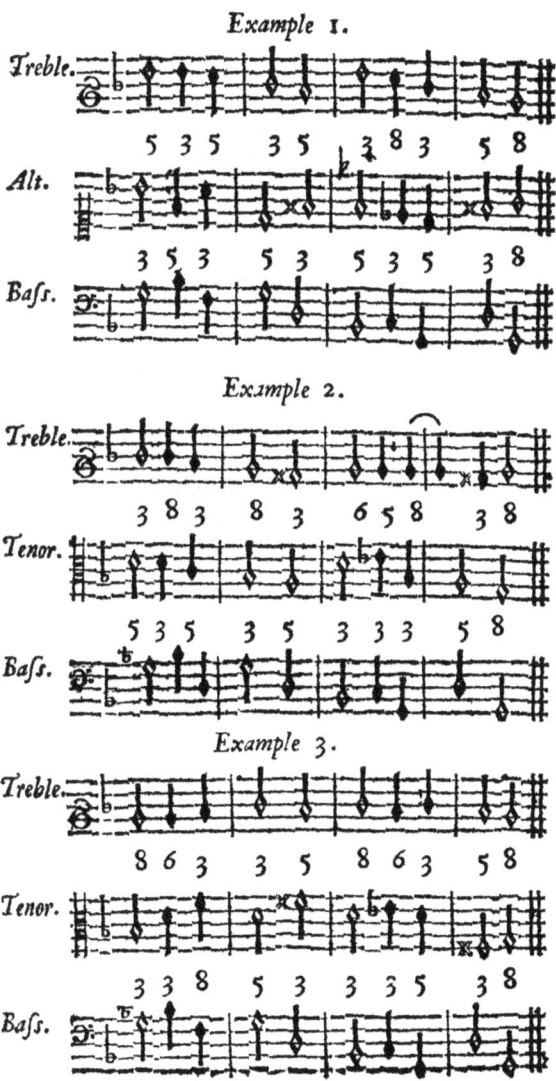

Example 2.

Example 3.

That

A Compendium of Musick.

That ♭ *flat* which you see in the third Bar of all the three Examples of the Inner part, is set there to take away the harsh reflection of *E sharp* against ♭ *flat* the foregoing Note of the *Bass*: which is that we call *Relation Inharmonical*, of which I shall speak hereafter. As for the *Sharps* I refer you to what I said formerly of them: Only take notice that part of the *sharp 3d.* in the *Treble* Part of the second Example, is joyned to the foregoing Note, to make that Binding Cadence we formerly mentioned.

§ 10. *Composition of four Parts.*

IF you design your Composition for four Parts, I would then have you to joyn your *Alt* as near as you can to the *Treble*; which is easily done by taking those Concords (Note after Note) which are next under the *Treble*, in manner as follows.

Example.

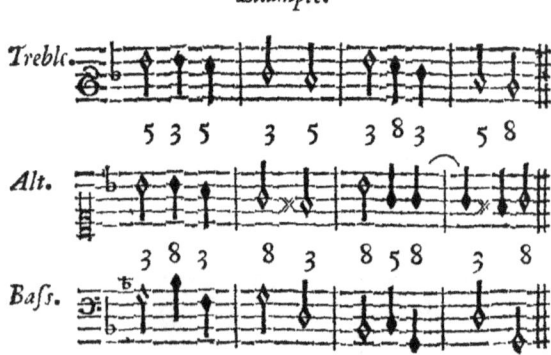

Principles of Composition. 45

I make the *Alt* and *Treble* end both in the same Tone; which, in my opinion, is better than to have the *Treble* end in the *sharp* 3*d.* above, the Key of the Composition being *flat*, and the *sharp* 3*d.* more proper for an Inward part at Conclusion.

I will now, by adding another Part (*viz.* a *Tenor*) shew you the accomplishment of Four Parts: concerning which, these Rules are to be observed.

First, that this Part which is to be added, be set in Concords different from the other two upper Parts. That is to say, if those be a 5*th*. and 3*d*. let this be an 8*th*; by which you may conceive the rest.

Secondly, I would have you joyn this *Tenor* as near the *Alt* as the different Concords do permit; for the Harmony is better when the three upper Parts are joyned close together.

Thirdly, you are to avid two 8*ths*. or two 5*ths*. rising or falling together, as well amongst the upper Parts, as betwixt any one Part and the *Bass*, of which there is less danger, by placing the Parts in different Concords.

Example.

48 *A Compendium of Musick.*

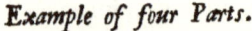

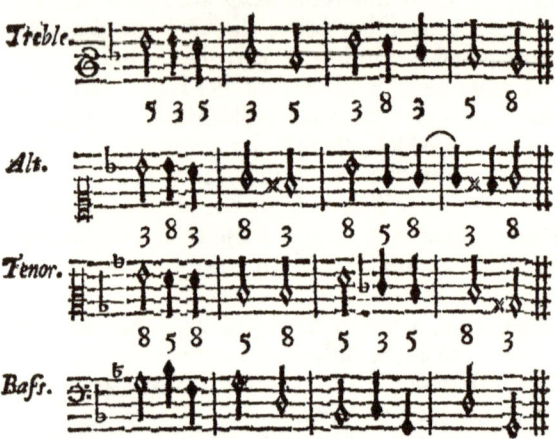

Here you may perceive each Note of the newly added *Tenor*, set in a Concord still different from those of the other two higher Parts, by which the Composition is compleated in four Parts. And though I have shewed this Composition, by adding one Part after another, which I did conceive to be the easiest way of giving you a clear understanding of it; yet, now that you know how to place the Concords, it is left to your liberty to carry on your Parts (so many as you design) together, and to dispose them into several Concords, as you shall think convenient.

§ 11. *How*

Principles of Composition. 47

§ 11. *How a* 5th. *and* 6th. *may stand together in* Counterpoint.

IT is generally delivered by most Authors which I have seen, that how many Parts soever a Composition consists of, there can be but three several Concords joyned at once, to any one Note of the *Bass*; that is to say, either a *3d.* *5th.* and *8th.* or a *3d.* *6th.* and *8th*; and, that when the *5th.* takes place, the *6th.* is to be omitted; and contrarily, if the *6th.* be used, the *5th.* is to be left out.

Our excellent and worthy Countryman Mr. *Thomas Morley*, in his *Introduction to Musick*, pag. 143. teaching his Scholar to compose four Parts, useth these words, *But when you put in a* 6th. *then of force must the* 5th. *be left out*; *except at a Cadence or Close where a Discord is taken*, thus:

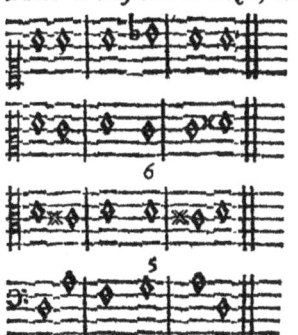

which is the best manner of closing, and the only way of taking a 5th *and* 6th *together*.

All this is to be understood as speaking of a *perfect* 5th. But there is another 5th. in Musick, called a false, defective, or imperfect *5th*; which necessarily requires a *6th.* to be joyned with it: And though I never heard any approved Author accompt it for a Concord, yet is it of most excellent use in Composition; and hath a particular grace and elegancy, even in this plain way of Counterpoint. It is commonly produced by making the lower

48   *A Compendium of Musick.*

lower term or *Bass-Note, sharp*, as you see in the two Instances following.

Thus you see how a **5th.** and **6th.** may be used at once; In any other way than these I have mention'd I do not conceive how they can stand together in Counterpoint, but when one of them is put in, the other is to be left out, according to the common Rule.

§ 12. *Composition in a sharp Key.*

WE will now proceed to a *sharp* Key; in which, *6ths.* are very frequent, for there are certain *sharp* Notes of the *Bass*, which necessarily require a lesser *6th.* to be joyned to them: As namely, 1. The Half-Note, or *lesser* 2*d.* under the Key of the Composition. 2. The *greater* 3*d.* above the Key. 3. Also the 3*d.* under it, requiring somtimes the *greater*, and somtimes the *lesser* 6*th.* to be joyned to it, as you see in the subsequent Example, in which the Notes of the *Bass* requiring a *6th.* are marked with little Crosses under them.

Treble

Principles of Composition. 49

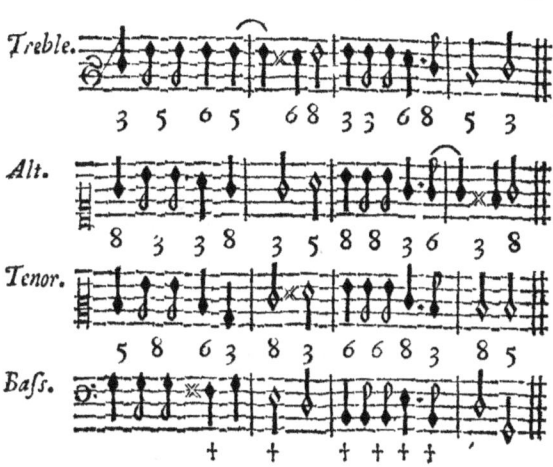

Things to be noted in this Example are these: 1. When the Notes of the *Bass* keep still in the same place, it is left to your liberty to remove the other Parts as you shall think fit: An Instance whereof you have in the next Notes after the beginning. 2. Take notice (and observe it hereafter) that the Half-Note or *sharp* Second under the Key, doth hardly admit an 8th. to be joyned to it, without offence to a critical Ear; and therefore have I joyned two 6ths. and a 3d. to that *sharp* Note of the *Bass* in F. 3. In the first part of the second Bar, you may see the *Treble* lending part of its 6th. to the foregoing Note, to make that Binding Cadence which we formerly mention'd. *pag.* 41. 4. You may observe that now I permit the *Treble* to end in a *sharp* 3d. which I did not approve when the Key was *flat*.

The Figures shew you which Parts are 6ths. to the *Bass*, as the marks, which Notes of the *Bass* require them: where you must know, that the *Bass*,

E

50 *A Compendium of Musick.*

in all such like Notes, doth assume the nature of an upper Part, wanting commonly a 3*d*, sometimes a 5*th*. of that Latitude or Compass which is proper to the true nature of a *Bass*.

To demonstrate this, we will remove the said Notes into their proper Compass; and then you will see those *6ths*. changed into other Concords, the upper Parts remaining the same they were, or else using those Notes which the *Bass* assumed before.

Example.

Here you may perceive, that by removing those Notes of the *Bass* a 3*d*. lower, all the *6ths*. are taken away, except that *5th*. which made the Binding Cadence: and that also will be taken quite away, if we remove its *Bass-Note* into its full Latitude, which is a 5*th*. lower; as you will easily see by the Instance next following.

By

Principles of Composition. 51

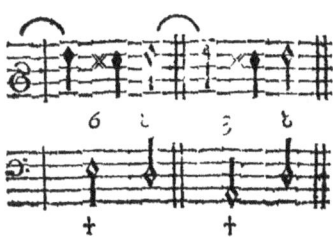

By this which hath been shewed, you see where *6ths* are to be used in Composition, and how they may be avoided when you please. But I would have you take notice, that *Basses consisting much of Notes which require 6ths. to be joyned to them, are more apt for few, than for many Parts.* The like may be said of *basses* that move much by Degrees.

§ 13. *Of Transition, or Breaking a Note.*

ONe thing yet remains, very necessary (sometimes) in Composition: and that is, to make smooth or sweeten the roughness of a Leap, by a gradual Transition to the Note next following, which is commonly called the *Breaking of a Note.* The manner of it you have in the following Examples, where the *Minim* in B, is broken to a 3*d*. 4*th*. and 5*th*. both downward and upward.

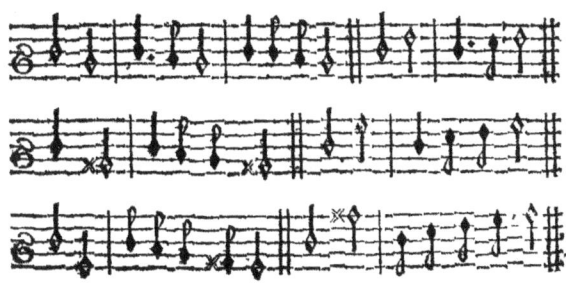

In like manner may a *Semibreve* be broken into smaller Notes. Where take notice also, that two,

E 2 three,

three, or more Notes, standing together in the same Line or Space may be considered as one intire Note; and consequently capable of Transition.

Example.

In which, you have no more to take care of, but that the first Particle express the Concord, and that the last produce not two 5*ths*. or 8*ths*. with some other Part. To avoid which (if it so happen) the following Note of the other Part may be altered, or the Transition may be omitted.

We will take the late Example with its 6*ths*. and apply some of these Breakings to such Notes as do require them, or may admit them.

Example.

Treble.

Alt.

Tenor.

Bass.

The

Principles of Compoſition. 53

The Breakings are marked with little Stars under them; which you will better conceive if you caſt your Eye back upon their original Notes.

In this I have made the *Treble* and *Alt.* end both in the ſame Tone, that you might ſee the *Tenor* fall by Tranſition into the *Greater* 3*d.* at the Cloſe.

Theſe Rules and Inſtructions which I have now delivered, being duly obſerved, may (I doubt not) ſuffice to ſhew you what is neceſſary for Compoſition of Two, Three, or Four Parts, in Counterpoint.

I have ſet my Examples all in the ſame Key, (*viz.* in G) that I might give the leſs diſturbance to your apprehenſion; which being once confirmed, you may ſet your Compoſitions in what Key you pleaſe, having regard to the *Greater* and *Leſſer* 3*d.* as hath been ſhewed.

§ 14. *Compoſition of* 5, 6, *and* 7 *Parts.*

BY that which hath been ſhewed, it plainly appears, that there can be but three different Concords applyed at once to any one Note of the Baſs, that is to ſay, (generally ſpeaking) either a 3*d.* 5*th.* and 8*th.* or a 3*d.* 6*th.* and 8*th.* Hence it follows, that if we joyn more Parts than three to the *Baſs*, it muſt be done by doubling ſome of thoſe Concords. *v. g.* If one Part more be added, which makes a Compoſition of Five Parts, ſome one of the ſaid Concords muſt ſtill be doubled. If two be added, which makes a Compoſition of ſix Parts, the duplication of two of the Concords will be required. If Three Parts more be added, which makes up Seven Parts; then all the three Concords will be doubled. And conſequently, the more Parts a Compoſition conſiſts of, the more redoublings of the Concords will be required. Which redoublings muſt be either in their *Octaves*, or in their *Uniſons.*

E 3 I

54   *A Compendium of Musick.*

I mention *Unisons*, because many Parts cannot stand within the Compass of the Scale of Musick, but some of those Parts must of necessity meet somtimes in *Unison*.

That I may explicate these things more clearly, I will set you Examples of 5, 6, and 7 Parts, with such observations as may occur therein: And being able to joyn so many Parts together in *Counterpoint*, you will find less difficulty to compose them in Figurate Descant, because there you will have more liberty to change or break off upon the middle of a Note.

Example of Five Parts.

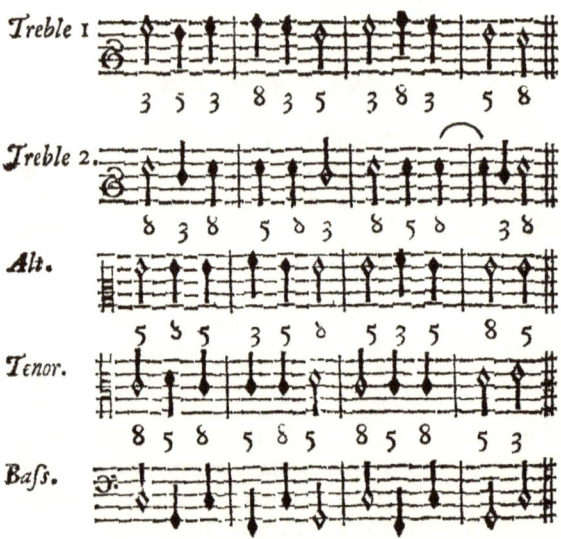

Here you see some one of the Concords still doubled, as may be observed by the Figures which denote them. Your next shall be of Six Parts; wherein two Concords will still be doubled to each Note of the *Bass.*

Exam-

Principles of Composition. 55

Example of Six Parts.

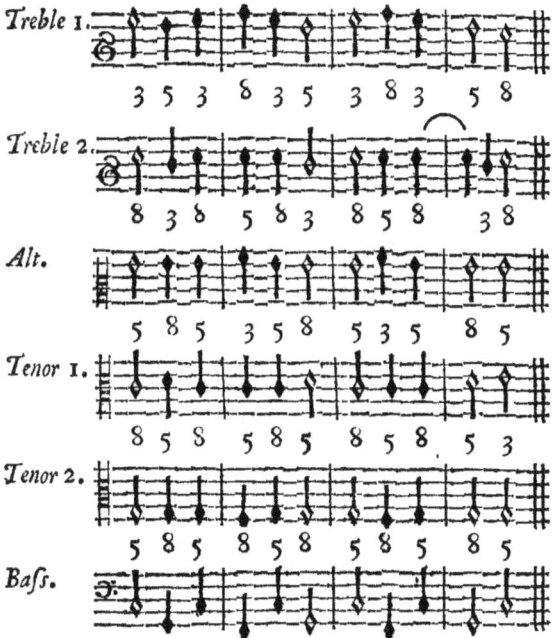

Here you see two Concords doubled, in which, all you have to observe is, how they remove several ways, the one upward, the other downward, by which means they avoid the Confecution of Perfects of the same kind.

A Compendium of Musick.

Example of Seven Parts.

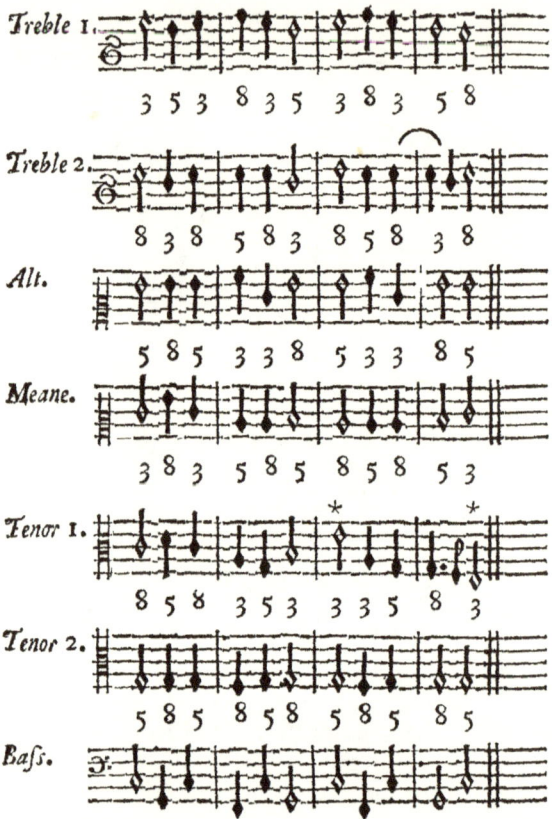

Obfervations in this Example are thefe. Firſt, that all the three Concords are, either doubled, or if any one ſtand ſingle, (as that which makes the Binding Cadence muſt always do) it doth neceſſitate ſome other Concord to be trebled. Secondly, that though the Parts do meet ſometimes in *Uniſon*
when

Principles of Composition. 57

when it cannot be avoided, yet they must not remain so, longer than necessity requires. Lastly, take notice, that the Notes of one Part may be placed above or below the Notes of another neighbouring Part, either to avoid the Consecution of Perfects, or upon any voluntary design. The Notes so transposed are marked with little stars over them, that you may take better notice of them.

§ 15. *Of two Basses, and Composition of Eight Parts.*

MAny Compositions are said to have two *Basses*, (because they are exhibited by two Viols or Voices) when, in reality they are both but one *Bass* divided into several parcels, of which, either *Bass* doth take its Part by turns, whilst the other supplys the office of another Part. Such are commonly design'd for Instruments. But here we are to speak of two *Basses* of a different nature; and that in reference to Composition of Eight Parts; which, whether intended for Church or Chamber, is usually parted into two Quires; either Quire having its peculiar *Bass*, with three upper Parts thereto belonging.

These two Quires answer each other by turns: sometimes with a single voice, sometimes with two, three, or all four; more or less, according to the subject, matter, or fancy of the Composer. But when both Quires joyn together, the Composition consists of Eight Parts, according to the following Example. In which you will see two *Basses*, either of them moving according to the nature of that Part, and either of them also, if set alone, a true *Bass* to all the upper Parts of either Quire; for such ought the two *Basses* to be, which here I do mean.

And

A Compendium of Musick.

And though it be a thing which few of our chief Composers do observe, yet I cannot but deliver my opinion therein, leaving the skilful to follow which way they most affect.

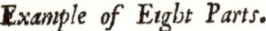

Example of Eight Parts.

Principles of Composition.

As concerning the Concordance of these two *Basses* betwixt themselves, it must be, in every respective Note, either an *Octave*, an *Unison*, a *Third*, or a *Sixth*, one to the other: not a *Fifth*, because the upper *Bass* (being set alone, or sounding louder than the other) will be a 4*th.* to all those upper Parts which were *Octaves* to the lower *Bass*. But where the *Basses* are a 3*d.* one to the other, if you take away the lower *Bass*, the 8*ths.* are only changed into 6*ths.* Again, if you take away the lower *Bass* where they are a 6*th.* one to the other; those upper Parts which were 6*ths.* to the lower *Bass*, will be 8*ths.* to the higher. Where the *Basses* sound in *Unison* or *Octave*, the upper Concords are the same to either.

The reason why I do not affect a 5*th.* betwixt the two *Basses* in Choral Musick is, that I would not have the Musick of one Quire to depend upon the *Bass* of the other, which is distant from it; but rather, that the Musick of either Quire be built upon its own proper *Bass*, and those two *Basses* with all their upper Parts to be such as may make one entire Harmony when they joyn together.

One thing more concerning two *Basses* is, that though they may often meet in 3*ds.* yet if they move successively in simple 3*ds.* they will produce a kind of buzzing, in low Notes especially, (as I have somtimes observed) which is not to be approved unless the Humour of the Words should require it.

What we have said of four Parts in a Quire, the same may be understood if either Quire consist of five or six voices. Also, if the Musick be composed for three or four Quires, each Quire ought to have its peculiar *Bass*, independent of the other: And the more Parts the Composition consists of when all are joyned together in a full *Chorus*; the greater
allow-

allowances may be granted: becaufe the multiplicity of voices doth drown or hide thofe little folecifmes which in fewer Parts would not be allowed.

This is as much as I think neceffary to be fhewed concerning *Counterpoint*, or plain *Defcant*, which is the Ground-work, or (as I may fay) the Grammar of Mufical Compofition. And though the Examples herein fet down (in which I have endeavoured no curiofity but plain inftruction) be fhort, fuitable to a *Compendium*, yet they are (I hope) fufficient to let you fee how to carry on your Compofitions to what length you fhall defire.

A

A COMPENDIUM
OF
PRACTICAL MUSICK.

THE THIRD PART,

TEACHING
The Use of Discords.

§ 1. *Concerning Discords.*

DIscords, as we formerly said of *Intervals* are *Indefinite*; for all *Intervals*, excepting those few which precisely terminate the Concords, are *Discords*. But our concernment in this place, is no more than with these that follow, *viz.* The *Lesser* and *Greater Second*. The *Lesser*, *Greater*, and *Perfect Fourth*. The *Lesser* or *Defective Fifth*. The *Lesser* and *Greater Seventh*. By these I also mean their *Octaves*.

§ 2. *How*

§ 2. *How Discords are admitted into Musick.*

Discords are two ways (chiefly used in Composition. First, in Diminution; That is, when two, three, or more Notes of one Part, are set against one Note of a different Part. And this is commonly done in making a gradual transition from one Concord to another; of which you had some intimation *pag.* 54. where I spoke of Breaking a Note.

In this way of passage, a *Discord* may be allowed in any one of the diminute Notes, except the first or leading Note, which ought always to be a Concord.

Example.

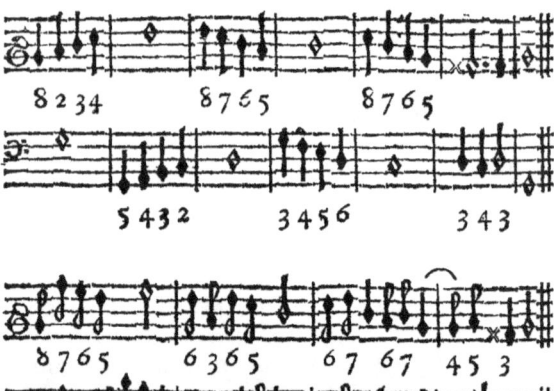

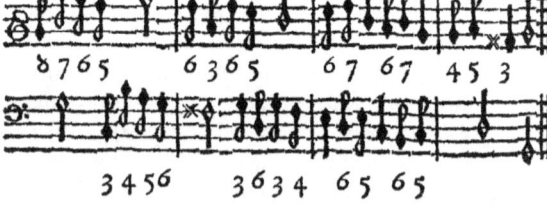

To which may be referred all kinds of Breakings or Dividings, either of the *Bass* it self, or of the *Descant* that is joyned to it; of which you may see
hun-

Use of Discords. 63

hundreds of Examples in my Book named *The Division Viol*, 3*d*. Part, the whole discourse being upon that Subject.

Here again take notice, that two, three, or more Notes standing together in the same line or space may be considered as one entire Note, and may admit a Discord to be joyned to any of them, the first only excepted.

Example.

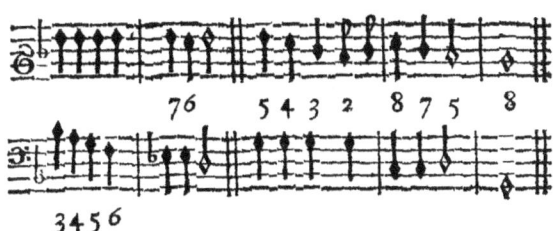

Although in this Example, I shew what liberty you have to use Discords; where many Notes stand together in the same line or space, which may properly be used in Vocal Musick, where both the Parts pronounce the same words or syllables together; yet it is not very usual in Musick made for Instruments.

§ 3. *Of Syncopation.*

THe other way in which Discords are not only allowed or admitted, but of most excellent use and Ornament in Composition, is, in Syncopation or Binding: That is, when a Note of one Part ends and breaks off upon the middle of the Note of another Part; as you see in the following Examples.

Syn-

A Compendium of Musick.

Syncopation in two Parts.

Syn-

Use of Discords. 63

Syncopation in three Parts.

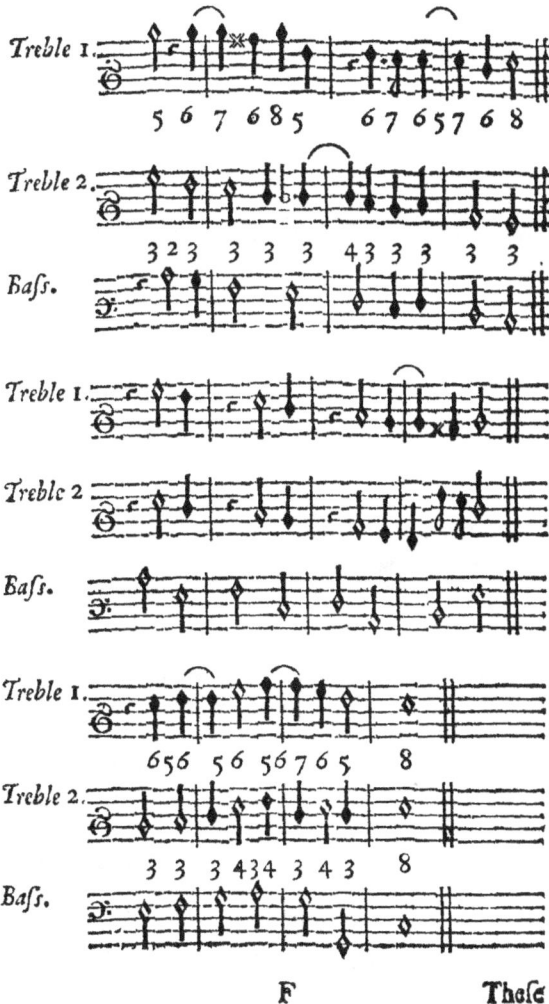

A Compendium of Musick.

Thefe Examples do fhew you all the Bindings or Syncopations that are ufually to be found: as 7*ths*. with 6*ths*, 6*ths*. with 5*ths*, 4*ths*. with 3*ds*, 3*ds*. with 2*ds*. Why 8*ths*. and 5*ths*. are exempt from Binding with their neighbouring Difcords, fhall prefently appear.

In this way of Binding, a Difcord may be applyed to the firft Part of any Note of the *Bafs*, if the other Part of the Binding-Note did found in concordance to that Note of the *Bafs* which went before, and fometimes alfo without that qualification, wherein fome Skill or Judgment is required.

§ 4. *Paffage of Difcords.*

Difcords thus admitted, we are next to confider how they are brought off, to render them delightful; for, fimply of themfelves they are harfh and difpleafing to the Ear, and introduced into Mufick only for variety, or, by ftriking the fenfe with a difproportionate found, to beget a greater attention to that which follows, to the hearing whereof we are drawn on (as it were) by a neceffary expectation.

This winding or bringing a Difcord off, is always beft effected by changing from thence into fome Imperfect Concord, to which more fweetnefs feems to be added by the Difcord founding before it. And here you have the Reafon why an 8*th*. and a 5*th*. do not admit of Syncopation or Binding, with their neighbouring Difcords: becaufe a 7*th*. doth Pafs more pleafingly into a 6*th*. as alfo a 9*th*. into a 10*th*. or 3*d*. And as for a 5*th*. though it Bind well enough with a 6*th*. (as you did fee in fome of the foregoing Examples) yet with a 4*th*. it will not Bind fo well, becaufe a 4*th*. doth Pafs more properly into a 3*d*.

Use of Discords.

These little windings and bindings with Discords and Imperfect Concords after them, do very much delight the Ear, yet do not satisfie it, but hold it in suspense (as it were) until they come to a perfect Concord, where (as at a Period) we understand the sense of that which went before.

Now, in passing from Discords to Imperfect Concords, we commonly remove to that which is nearest, rather than to one that is more remote; which Rule holds good also in passing from Imperfect Concords, to those that are more Perfect.

§ 5. *Of Discords, Note against Note.*

ALthough we have mention'd but two ways in which Discords are allowed, that is, in Diminution, and Syncopation; yet we find a third way, wherein Skilful Composers do often use them: which is, by setting Note for Note of the same quantity one against another. And though it be against the Common Rules of Composition; yet, being done with judgment and design, it may be ranked amongst the Elegances of Figurate Musick.

The prime or chief of which, for their use and excellency in Musick, are a *Tritone* and a *Semidiapente*; that is, the *Greater* or *Excessive* 4*th*. and the *Lesser* or *Defective* 5*th*. Which according to the Scale, where we have no other divisions or distinctions than *Semitones* or Half-Notes, seem to be the same *Interval*, as to proportion of sound, either of them consisting of six *Semitones*; but their appearance in practice is, one of them as a 4*th*, the other like a 5*th*; which, if placed one above the other, complete the compass of an *Octave*, in manner following.

Semidiapente.
Tritone.

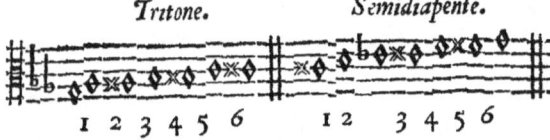
Tritone.   Semidiapente.
1 2 3 4 5 6   1 2 3 4 5 6

Their use in Figurate Descant is very frequent, both in Syncopation and Note against Note, as in *Counterpoint*. The *Tritone* passes naturally into a 6*th*. the *Semidiapente* into a 3*d*. thus:

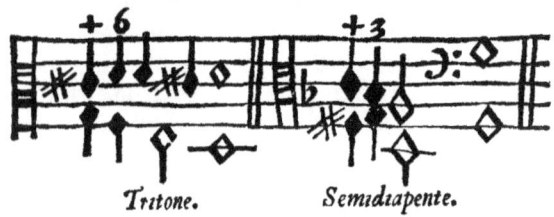
Tritone.   Semidiapente.

The Parts or Sounds which they usually require to be joyned with them, either in Binding or without it; are a Second above the lower Note of the *Tritone*; and a Second above the higher Note of the *Semidiapente*, which makes that 6*th*. we mention'd *p*.47. as necessary to be joyned with an *Imperfect* 5*th*.

Example.

Tritone.   Semidiapente.

§ 6. *Of Discords in double Transition.*

I Shewed you formerly, (*pag.* 51.) how a Note is sometimes broken to make a Transition by degrees to some other Concord.

These Transitions or Breakings are commonly express'd in *Quavers* or *Crochets*; somtimes (though seldom) in *Minims*. The Examples I gave you were set for the *Treble*, but may be applyed to the *Bass* also, or any other Part.

Now, if the *Bass* and an upper Part, do both make a Transition at the same time, in Notes of the same quantity, and in contrary motion, which is their usual Passage; there must (of necessity) be an encounter of Discords, whilst either Part proceeds by degrees towards its designed Concord. And therefore in such a Passage, Discords (no doubt) may be allowed Note against Note.

Example.

70   *A Compendium of Musick.*

Example.

Besides these which depend upon the Rule of Breaking and Transition, there may be other ways wherein a Skilful Composer may upon design set a Discord, for which no general Rule is to be given, and therefore, not to be exhibited to a Beginner; there being a great difference betwixt that which is done with judgment and design, and that which is committed by oversight or ignorance. Again, many things may be allowed in *Quavers* and *Crochets* (as in these Examples that I have shewed) which would not be so allowable in *Minims* or *Semibreves*.

I.

Use of Discords.

I told you formerly that Discords are best brought off, when they pass into *Imperfect* Concords: which is true Doctrine, and ought to be observed (as much as may be) in long Notes and Syncopation: But in short Notes and Diminution, we are not so strictly obliged to observance of that Rule. Neither can we Ascend or Descend by degrees to a 5*th.* or to an 8*th.* but a 4*th.* will come before the one, and a 7*th.* before the other.

Again, a 7*th.* doth properly pass into a 5*th.* when the Parts do meet in contrary motion, as you may see in the Example next following.

And here you may see two 7*ths.* both Parts Descending, betwixt the *Bass* and higher *Treble*; not by oversight, but set with design.

§ 7. *Of Relation Inharmonical.*

After this discourse of Discords, I think it very proper to say somthing concerning Relation Inharmonical, which I formerly did but only mention.

Relation, or **Respect**, or **Reference Inharmonical**, is a harsh reflection of *Flat* against *Sharp*, in a cross form; that is, when the present Note of one Part, compared with the foregoing Note of another Part, doth produce some harsh and displeasing Discord. Examples of it are such as follow:

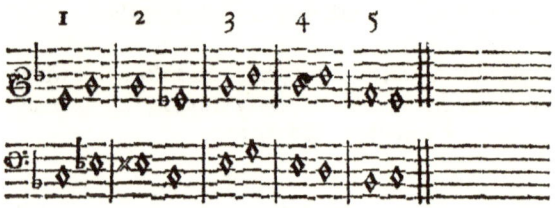

The first Note of the *Treble* is in *E sharp*, which considered (cross-wise) with the second Note of the *Bass* in *E flat*, begets the sound of a *Lesser Second*, which is a Discord. The second Example is the same Descending.

The third Example, comparing *E sharp* in the *Bass*, with *B flat* in the *Treble*, produces a false 5th, which is also a Discord. The like may be said of the fourth Example.

The first Note of the *Bass* in the fifth Example stands in *B flat*: which compared with the last Note of the *Treble*, in *E Sharp*, produces the sound of a *Tritone* or *Greater 4th*, which is also a harsh Discord.

Though these cross Relations sound not both together, yet they leave a harshness in the Ear, which is to be avoided, especially in Composition of few Parts.

But you must know, that this cross reflection of *Flat* against *Sharp*, doth not always produce Relation Inharmonical.

Example.

Use of Discords.

Example.

For it is both usual and proper for the upper Part to change from *flat* to *sharp* when the *Bass* doth fall a *Lesser* 3 *d.* as you see in the first and second Bars of this Example. Also that reflection of *F sharp* against ♮ *flat*, in the third Bar, which produces the sound of a *Lesser* 4*th.* is not Relation Inharmonical. The reason thereof you shall presently have. But first I will give you a clearer Instance thereof, by comparing it with another 4*th.* *flat* against *sharp* cross-wise, that your own Ear may better judge what is, and what is not, Relation Inharmonical.

Example.

The first two Instances shew a Relation of *F sharp* in the *Bass*, against *B flat* in the *Treble*, which begets the sound of a *Lesser* 4*th.* and is very good
and

and usual in Composition. The other two Instances are *F flat* in the *Bass*, against *B sharp* in the *Treble*, which makes a *Greater* or *Excessive* 4th. a very harsh Relation. And here (by the way) you may observe three different 4ths. in Practical Musick. *viz.* 1. From *F sharp* to *B flat* upward, 2. From *F Flat* to *B flat*; and 3. From *F flat* to *B sharp*, thus exemplified.

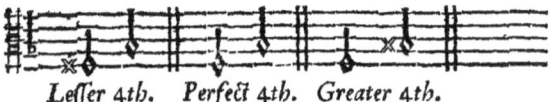

Lesser 4th.   *Perfect* 4th.   *Greater* 4th.

As to the reason, why *F sharp* against ♭ *flat* doth not produce Relation Inharmonical, we are to consider the proportion of its *Interval*, which (indeed) belongs rather to the Theory of Musick : for though the Ear informs a Practical Composer, which sounds are harsh or pleasing, it is the speculative Part that considers the Reason why such or such *Intervals* make those sounds which please or displease the Ear.

But we will reduce this business of the *Lesser* 4th. into Practice ; that thereby we may give a reason to a Practical Musician why it falls not under Relation Inharmonical. To which purpose we will examine it according to our common Scale of Musick, and there we shall find it to consist of no more than four *Semitones* or Half-Notes; which is the very same number that makes a *Ditone*, or *Greater* 3*d*. Example will render it more plain.

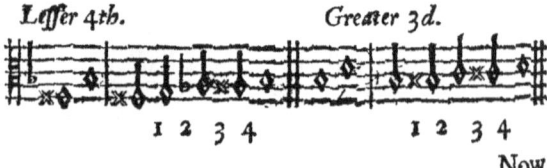

Now

Use of Discords.

Now I suppose that no Practical Musician will say that the two Terms of a *Greater 3d.* have any harsh Relation one to the other, which granted, doth also exempt the other (being the like *Interval*) from Relation Inharmonical, though in appearance it be a *4th.* and hath *flat* against *sharp* in a cross reflection.

By this you may perceive that distances in the Scale, are not always the same in sound, which they seem to the sight. To illustrate this a little further, we will add a *Lesser 3d.* to the former *Lesser 4th.* which in appearance will make a *Lesser 6th.* for so the degrees in the Scale will exhibit it, in manner following.

4th. 3d.   6th.   6th.

But this *6th.* in sight, is no more in sound than a common *5th.* which we may demonstrate by the Scale it self: For, if we remove each Term a *Semitone* lower (which must needs keep them still at the same distance) we shall find the *6th.* changed into a *5th.* in sight as well as found, and the *Lesser 4th.* likewise changed into a *Greater 3d.* as you may see in this Example.

And if we remove the latter three Notes again, and set them a *Semitone* higher by adding a *sharp* to each Note, thus, that which in the first Instance was *D flat*, is now become *C sharp*; and likewise *B flat* now changed into *A sharp*.

This removing of the Concords a *Semitone* higher or lower, as also the changing them into Keys which have

have no affinity with the Cardinal Key upon which the Aire of the Musick dependeth, does many times cause an Untunableness in the Concords, as though our Strings were out of Tune when we Play upon Instruments which have fixed Stops or *Frets*: And this also happens amongst the Keys of Harpsecords, and Organs, the reason whereof is, the inequality of *Tones* and *Semitones*, either of them having their *Major* and *Minor*, which our common Scale doth not distinguish. And this has caused some to complain against the Scale it self, as though It were defective. Concerning which I will presume no further than the delivering of my own opinion, to which purpose I must first say somthing

§ 8. *Of the three Scales of Musick.*

THe three Scales are these. 1. *Scala Diatonica.* 2. *Scala Cromatica.* 3. *Scala Enharmonica.* The *Diatonick* Scale, is that which rises to a 5*th.* by three *Tones* and a *Semitone*, and from thence to the 8*th.* by two *Tones* and one *Semitone*: which *Semitone* is denoted in both places by *Fa*, as I shewed in the beginning of this Treatise.

Example.

This is (in effect) the Old *Grecian* Scale, consisting of four *Tetrachords* or 4*ths.* extending to a double *Octave*, which *Guido Aretinus*, a Monk of St. *Benedict*'s Order (about the year of our Lord 960.) changed

Use of Discords.

changed into a form in which it now is; setting this *Greek* letter Γ *Gamma* at the bottom of it, to acknowledge from whence he had it: and This (for its general use) is now called the Common Scale of Musick.

The *Chromatick* Scale rises to a 5*th*. by a *Tone* and five *Semitones*, and from thence proceeds to an 8*th*. by five *Semitones* more.

Example.

Some perhaps may find fault with this Example of the *Chromatick* Scale, as being not the usual way of setting it down: but I thought it the best Instance I could give a Learner of it, as to its use in Practical Musick; In which it is so frequently mixed with the *Diatonick* Scale, that the ♭ *flat* and ♯ *sharp* which formerly belonged to *B* only, have now got the names of the *Chromatick* Signs, by their frequent application to Notes in all places of the Scale: and the Musick which moves much in *Semitones* or Half-Notes, is commonly called *Chromatick* Musick. And from hence it is that an *Octave* is divided into 12 *Semitones*.

The *Enharmonick* Scale rises gradually by *Dëïses* or Quarter-Notes, of which 24 make up an *Octave:* and is so far out of use, that we scarce know how to give an *Example* of it Those who endeavour it, do set it down in this manner,

But

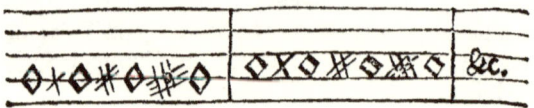

But, as to its use, in Practical Musick, I am yet to seek. For I do not conceive how a natural Voice can Ascend or Descend by such Minute degrees, and hit them right in Tune. Neither do I see how Syncopes or Bindings with Discords (which are the chief ornaments of Composition) can be performed by Quarter-Notes. Or, how the Concords (by them) can be removed from Key to Key, without much trouble and confusion. For these reasons I am slow to believe that any good Musick (especially of many Parts) can be composed by Quarter-Notes, although I hear some talk much of it.

Only one place there is, where I conceive a Quarter-Note might serve instead of a *Semitone*, which is, in the Binding Cadence of the *Greater* 3d. and That, commonly, is covered or drowned either by the *Trill* of the Voice, or *shake* of the Finger.

But some do fancy, that as the *Diatonick* Scale is made more elegant by a Mixture of the *Chromatick* so likewise it might be bettered by help of the *Enharmonick* Scale, in such places where those little Dissonances do occur.

I do not deny but that the slitting of the Keys in *Harpsecords* and *Organs*, as also the placing of a **Middle Fret** near the Top or Nut of a Viol or *Theorbo*, where the space is wide may be useful in some cases, for the sweetning of such Dissonances as may happen in those places: but I do not conceive that the *Enharmonick* Scale is therein concerned, seeing those Dissonances are sometimes more, sometimes less, and seldom that any of them do hit precisely the Quarter of a Note. Now,

Use of Discords.

Now, as to my opinion concerning our common Scale of Musick; taking it with its mixture of the *Chromatick*; I think it lies not in the wit of man to frame a better, as to all intents and purposes for Practical Musick. And, as for those little Dissonances (for so I call them, for want of a better word to express them) the fault is not in the Scale, whose office and design is no more than to denote the distances of the Concords and Discords, according to the Lines and Spaces of which it doth consist; and to shew by what degrees of *Tones* and *Semitones* a Voice may rise or fall.

For in Vocal Musick those Dissonances are not perceived, neither do they occur in Instruments which have no *Frets*, as *Violins* and wind Instruments, where the sound is modulated by the touch of the Finger, but in such only as have fixed Stops or *Frets*; which, being placed and fitted for the most usual Keys in the Scale, seem out of order when we change to Keys less usual; and that (as I said) doth happen by reason of the inequality of *Tones* and *Semitones*, especially of the latter.

Concerning which, I shall (with submission to better judgments) adventure to deliver my own sense and opinion. And though it belongs more properly to the Mathematick Part of Musick, yet (happily) a Practical explication thereof may give some satisfaction to a Practical Musician, when he shall see and understand the Reason.

§ 9. *Of Greater and Lesser* Semitones.

First, you must know, that Sounds have their Proportions as well as Numbers.

Those Proportions may be explicated by a line divided into 2, 3, 4, 5, or more equal Parts. We will suppose that line to be the String of a *Lute* or *Viol*. Take which String you please, so it be true; but the smallest is fittest for the purpose.

Divide the length of that String, from the Nutt to the Bridge, into two equal Parts; stop it in the Middle, and you will hear the Sound of an *Octave*, if you compare it with the Sound of the open String. Therefore is a *Diapason* said to be in *dupla* proportion to its *Octave*.

Next, divide the String into three equal parts, and stop that part next the Nutt, (which will be at the *Fret* [*b*] if rightly placed) compare the Sound thereof with the open String, and you will hear the difference to be a 5*th*. Thence is a 5*th*. said to be *Sesquialtera* proportion; that is, as 2 is to 3.

Again, divide your String into four equal Parts, stop that Part next the Nutt (which will be, at the [*f*] *Fret*) and you have a 4*th*. to the open String. Therefore a 4*th*. is said to be *Sesquitertia* Proportion, as 3 is to 4. By these you may conceive the rest towards the Nutt.

If you ask me concerning the other half of the String from the middle to the Bridge: the middle of that half makes another *Octave*, and so every middle one after another.

We will now come a little nearer to our business of the *Semitones*. To which purpose we must divide the *Octave* it self into equal Parts. First, in the Middle, which will fall upon the *Fret* [*f*.] Examine the Sound from [*f*] to [*n*] (which is *Octave* to the open String) and you will find it to be a 5*th*. Try the other half which is towards the Nutt, and you will hear it is but a 4*th*.

Next, divide that 5*th*. which is from [*f*] to [*n*] into two equal Parts; and you will find That half, which is towards the Bridge, to be a *Greater* 3*d*. and and the other half to the Nutt-ward, to be a *Lesser* 3*d*.

Then

Use of Discords.

Then divide that *Greater* 3*d.* into two equal Parts, and you will have a *Greater* and a *Lesser Tone*. Lastly, divide that *Greater Tone* (which was that half next the *Bridge*) into two equal Parts, and you have a *Greater* and a *Lesser Semitone*; the *Greater* being always that half which is nearer to the Bridge.

By this you may perceive that all our Musical *Intervals* arise from the Division of a Line or String into equal Parts; and that those equal Parts, do still produce unequal Sounds. And this is the very Reason that we have *Greater* and *Lesser Semitones*.

Thereupon, is a *Tone*, or whole Note (as we term it) divided into Nine Particles, called *Comma's*: five of which are assigned to the *Greater Semitone*; and four to the *Less*. The difference betwixt them is called 'Ἀποτοµἱα, which signifies *a cutting off*. Some Authors call the *Greater Semitone*, *Apotome*; That is (I suppose) because it includes the odd *Comma* which makes that *Apotome*. Thus you see a *Tone* or Note divided into a *Greater* and *Lesser Half*, but, how to divide it into two equal Halfs, I never see determined.

The famous *Kircher* in his Learned and Elaborate *Musurgia Universalis*, pag. 103. treating of the Mathematick Part of Musick, (which he handles more clearly and largely than any Author (I think) that ever wrote upon that Subject) doth shew us the Type of a *Tone* cut in the middle by dividing the middle *Comma* into two *Schisms*. But that *Comma* (being divided Arithmetically) will have its *Greater* and a *Lesser* half (as to Sound) as well as any greater *Interval* so divided.

The nearest Instance I can give you of a Sound parted in the middle, is an *Octave*, divided into a *Tritone*, and a *Semidiapente*, either of them consisting of six *Semitones*, as I shewed *pag.* 68. and yet there is some little difference in their Rations or Habitudes:

G

I will give you yet a clearer Instance, by which you may see what different Sounds will arise, from one Division of a Line or String into equal Parts. To which purpose, divide that 5*th*. which is from the Nutt to [*h*] *Fret*, into two equal Parts, with a pair of Compasses ; (the middle whereof will hit upon [*d*] *Fret*,if it be not placed with some abatement, for the reasons forementioned ;) and you will find, that the same wideness of the Compass which divided the 5*th*. in the middle, and so made a *Greater* and a *Lesser* 3*d*. the same wideness (I say) applyed from [*h*] towards the Bridge, will, in the first place from [*h*] produce a 4*th*. in the next place, a 5*th*. and in the next after that, an 8*th*. according to this Line :

Nutt	Less 3*d*.	Great 3*d*.	Fourth	Fifth	Eight		Bridge
	a	*d*	*h*	*n*	*v*		

But seeing you cannot conveniently hear the Sound of that 8*th*. it being so near the Bridge ; take the wideness of the 5*th*. from the Nutt to [*h*] and you will find that the same wideness which makes a 5*th*. doth make an 8*th*. in the next place after it according to this Line :

Nutt	Fifth	Eight		Bridge
a	*h*	*v*		

If you please to try these distances upon the *Treble* String of a *Bass Viol*, you will have a production of these Sounds.

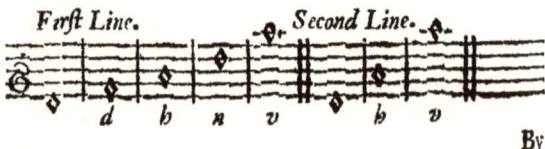

First Line.   Second Line.
d *h* *n* *v*   *h* *v*

Use of Discords.

By this you may perceive that every equal division of a Line or String, doth still produce a greater *Interval* of Sound, as it approaches nearer to the Bridge: And, by this which hath been shewed; I suppose you see not only the Reason, but Necessity, of *Greater* and *Lesser Semitones*. Our next business is to examine.

§ 10. *Where these Greater and Lesser Semitones arise in the Scale of Musick.*

This depends upon the Key in which a Song is sett, and upon the division of its 5*th*. into the *Greater* and *Lesser* 3*d*. and the placing of these, which determines whether the Key be *flat* or *sharp*, as hath been shewed. We will suppose the Key to be in *G*.

The *Diatonick* Scale hath only two places in each *Octave*, in which a *Semitone* takes place. One is in rising to the 5*th*. The other in rising from thence to the 8*th*. And these two places are known by the Note *fa*; as formerly shewed. These two Sounds denoted by *fa*, are always the *Lesser Semitone* from that degree which is next under them. So that from *A* to *B flat*, is a *Lesser Semitone*: and betwixt *B flat* and *B sharp* (which makes the difference of the *Lesser* and *Greater* 3*d*.) is (or ought to be) always the *Greater Semitone*. The like may be understood of the higher *fa*.

I know that some Authors do place the *Greater Semitone* from *A* to *B flat*, and the *Lesser* betwixt *B flat* and *B sharp*, but I adhere to the other opinion, as the more rational to my understanding.

By this you see where *Greater* and *Lesser Semitones* take place in the *Diatonick* Scale. We will now cast our Eye upon them as they rise in the *Chromatick*; according to the Example I gave you of it. In which, the *Greater* and *Leſſer* Half-Notes do follow each other ſucceſſively, as ſhall be here denoted by two letters, *l* for *Leſſer*, and *g* for *Greater*:

Example.

Now, if we ſhould remove this Example a *Semitone* higher or lower; the *Leſſer Semitones* would fall in the places of the *Greater*, and contrarily, the *Greater* in the places of the *Leſſer*: which tranſpoſition, is the chief cauſe of thoſe little Diſſonances, which occaſion'd this diſcourſe.

Your beſt way to avoid them, is, to ſet your Muſick in the uſual and moſt natural Keys of the Scale.

A COMPENDIUM OF PRACTICAL MUSICK.

THE FOURTH PART,

TEACHING

The Form of Figurate Descant.

§ 1. *What is meant by Figurate Descant.*

Figurate Descant is that wherein Discords are concerned as well as Concords. And, as we termed Plain Descant, (in which was taught the use of the Concords) The Ground-work or Grammar of Musical Composition, so may we as properly nominate This, the Ornament or Rhetorical Part of Musick. For, in This are introduced all the varieties of Points, Fuges, Syncope's or Bindings, Diversities of Measures, Intermixtures of discording Sounds, or what else Art and Fancy can exhibit; which, as different Flowers and Figures, do set forth and adorn the Composition, whence it is named *Melothesa florida vel figurata*, Florid or Figurate Descant.

§ 2. *Of the* Greek *Moods, and* Latin *Tones.*

BEfore we treat of Figurate Descant, I must not omit to say somthing concerning the Moods or Tones. Not so much for any great use we have of them, as to let you know what is meant by them, and that I may not appear singular, for you shall scarce meet with any Author that has writ of Musick, but you will read somthing concerning them.

The Moods we mention'd in the first Part of this Treatise, were in reference to Notes, and Measure of Time. These are concerning Tune.

That which the *Grecians* called Mode or Mood, the *Latins* termed Tone or Tune. The design of either was, to shew in what Key a Song was sett, and which Keys had affinity one with another. The *Greeks* distinguished their Moods by the names of their Provinces; as *Dorick, Lidian, Ionick, Phrigian, &c.* The *Latins* reduced theirs, to eight Plainsong Tunes, and those were set in the *Tenor*. so called, because it was the Holding Part to which they did apply their Descant.

These Plain-songs did seldom exceed the Compass of six Notes or degrees of Sound: and therefore were *Ut* and *Re* (as I suppose) appled to the two lowest, that each degree might have a several appellation: otherwise, four names, as now we use, viz. *Mi, Fa, Sol, La,* had been both more easie, and more suitable to the ancient Scale, which consisted of *Tetrachords* or *4ths*. two of which made up the Compass of an *Octave.*

From these six Notes, *Ut, Re, Mi, Fa, Sol, La,* did arise three properties of Singing; which they
named

Figurate Descant.

named *B Quarre*, *B Molle*, and *Properchant* or *Natural*. *B Quarre*, was when the Sung *Mi* in *B*; that Cliff being then made of a Square form thus, ♮ and set at the beginning of the Lines, as we now set some one of the other three *Cliffs*. *B Molle* was when they Sung *Fa* in *B*. *Properchant* was when their *Ut* was applyed to *C*, so that their six Notes did not reach so high as to touch *B* either *flat* or *sharp*. But in our modern Musick, we acknowledge no such thing as *Properchant*; every Song being, of its own nature, either *flat* or *sharp*: and that determin'd (not by *B*'s *flat* or *sharp*, but) by the *Greater* or *Lesser* 3*d*. being joyned next to the Key in which any Song is set.

These Moods or Tones had yet another distinction; and that was *Authentick*, or *Plagal*. This depended upon the dividing of the *Octave* into its 5*th*. and 4*th*. *Authentick* was when the 5*th*. stood in the lower place, according to the Harmonical division of an *Octave*. *Plagal*, was when the 5*th*. possest the upper place, according to the Arithmetical division thereof.

Example.

Authentick.   *Plagal.*

Harmonical.   *Arithmetical.*

Many Volumes have been wrote about these Moods or Tones, concerning their use, their number, nature and affinity one with another; and yet the business left imperfect or obscure, as to any certain Rule for regulating the Key and Air of the Musick, though one of the greatest concernments of Musical Composition.

Mr. *Morley* (upon this Subject) in his *Introduction*

ction to Musick, pag. 147. his Scholar making this Quærie, *Have you no general Rule to be given for an instruction for keeping of the Key?* answers, *No*, *for it must proceed only of the judgment of the Composer*, yet (saith he) *the Church-men for keeping of their Keys have devised certain Notes commonly called the eight Tunes*, &c. of which he only gives Examples, and so leaves the business. And no marvel they could give no certain Rule, so long as they took their light from the *Tenor*, in which case it must of necessity be left to the judgment of the Composer or Singer of Descant, what *Bass* he will apply unto it. But, according to the Method formerly deliver'd in this Treatise, where we make the *Bass* the foundation of the Harmony, upon which the Key solely depends, as also the other Keys which have affinity therewith, the business is reduced to a certainty of Rule, both plain and easie. (see *pag*. 34. Concerning the Key or Tone.) And though in Figurate Descant we often have occasion to apply under-Notes to an upper Part, as you will see hereafter, yet the whole conduct of the Composition, as to the Key and middle Closes thereto belonging, is the very same, and therefore to be observed, according to what we there delivered.

I give you this brief account of the *Moods* and *Tones*, that you might not be wholly ignorant of any thing that belongs to Musick: To which purpose I have contrived this little Table: collected out of such Authors as number 12 Tones or Tunes answerable to the *Grecian Moods*; viz. six *Authentick*, and six *Plagal*.

		Authentick.		Plagal.
D	1	Dorick	2	Hypo-Dorick
E	3	Phrygian	4	Hypo-Phrygian
F	5	Lydian	6	Hypo-Lydian
G	7	Mixolydian	8	Hypo-Mixolydian
A	9	Æolian	10	Hypo-Æolian
C	11	Ionick	12	Hypo-Ionick

Figurate Descant.

The first Column shews the Keys in the Scale of Musick to which those Tones and Moods are assigned. The second expresses the order of the *Authentick* Tones, known by their odd Numbers, as 1, 3, 5, &c. The third Column contains the names of the *Grecian Authentick* Moods. The fourth shews the *Plagal* Tones, known always by their even numbers, as 2, 4, 6, &c. The last or fifth Column contains the names of the *Grecian Plagal* Moods, distinguished by the Particle *Hypo*.

Where you may observe, that B *mi*, is exempt from having any Tone or Mood assigned to it, because F *fa*, doth make an *Imperfect* 5th. thereto. Howbeit, B *fa*, is become a Key or Tone now much in use, especially in Musick composed for Instruments.

But, whereas we read such strange and marvellous things of the various affections and different effects of the *Grecian* Moods, we may very probably conjecture that it proceeded chiefly from their having Moods of different measure joyned with them; which, we find by experience, doth make that vast difference betwixt Light and Grave Musick; though both set in the same Key, and consequently the same Mood or Tone.

§ 3. *Of Figurate Musick in general.*

Figurate Descant (as I told you) is that wherein Discords are concerned as well (though not so much) as Concords. You have already been taught the use of both in Composition, and These are the Two Materials which must serve you for the raising of all Structures in Figurate Musick.

To give you Models at large, of all those several Structures, were to write a great Volume, not a *Compendium*. It will be sufficient that I let you see the Form of Figurate Descant; and that I give you some short Examples of such things as are of most concernment; with Instructions (so near as I can) for their contrivance. We will begin with setting a *Bass* to a *Treble*, as we formerly did with making a *Treble* to a *Bass*.

§ 4. *How to sett a* Bass *to a* Treble.

IN this you must reckon your Concords from the *Treble* downward, as in the other you did from the *Bass* upward. Which is but the same thing in effect, for, a *3d. 5th. 6th.* and *8th.* are still the same, whether you reckon them upward or downward.

But, whereas in plain *Counterpoint*, I did order the *Bass* to move on, for the most part, by leaps of a 3, 4, 5, &c. (which indeed is the most proper movement of the *Bass* in that kind of Composition,) here you must know, that in Figurate Descant, those leaps are frequently changed or broken into degrees; as you may easily conceive by this Example:

And therefore it is left to your liberty to use either the one or the other as occasion shall require. Only take notice, that if (in these Breakings) the Parts do Ascend or Descend together by degrees, it must be either in *3ds.* or *6ths.* If they move contrary by degrees, (that is, one rising, the other falling) you have liberty to pass through Discords as well as
Con-

Figurate Descant. 91

Concords, according to what I shewed of Discords Note against Note. For the rest I refer you to the Principles formerly delivered in Composition of two Parts. And if your *Treble* do chance to hold out any long Note, you may let the *Bass*, during the time, pass on from one *Imperfect* Concord to another; as from a 3*d.* to a 6*th.* or the contrary. The like may be understood of the *Treble*, when the *Bass* holds out a Note.

Also your Composition will be more neat, if you can use some formality in your *Bass*, by imitating and answering the Notes of the *Treble* in such places as will admit it.

We will now suppose a *Treble* made by some other person, as, indeed, this was, which I am about to Prick down (made by a Person of Quality) and given to have a *Bass* sett to it.

Example.

A Compendium of Musick.

Example of a Bass *made to a* Treble.

Here

Figurate Descant.

Here you see the *Bass* still answering and imitating the *Treble*, (so near as the Rules of Composition do permit) sometimes in the *Octave*, as you see in most Part of the first Strain: and sometimes in other distances, as you may observe in the beginning of the second Strain: but still keeping close to the Rules of Composition, which must be chiefly observed. This is as much as I think necessary for setting a *Bass* to a *Treble*.

And by this you may perceive how different the Form and Movement of the Parts in Figurate Descant, is from that of plain *Counterpoint*: For, in That, the natural passage of the *Treble* is, for the most part by Degrees, In This, you may use what what Leaps you please, so they be airy and formal.

§ 5. *How Parts pass through one another.*

AGain, in *Counterpoint*, each Part does ordinarily move within its own Sphere. In Figurate Descant, the Parts do frequently mix and pass through one another: Insomuch, that if there be two *Trebles*, you shall have sometimes This, sometimes That, above or below, as you see in the following Instances.

The like may be understood of the Inner Parts, or of the *Basses*, when the Composition is designed for two. Howbeit the highest Part for the time being is still to be accounted the *Treble:* and the lowest Part, whatever it be, is (during that time) the *Bass* to all the Parts that stand above it.

Lastly, whereas in *Counterpoint* I commended unto you the joyning of your upper Parts so close together, that no other Part could be put in amongst them: in Figurate Musick, (especially for Instruments) that Rule is not so strictly observed, but each Part doth commonly move according to the Compass of the Voice or Instrument for which it is intended. But the Principles of Composition, as the choosing, ordering and placing of the Concords, are the very same we delivered in plain *Counterpoint:* that is to say, In two or three Parts you are to avoid 8*ths.* except in such places as there mentioned: In Four or more Parts you are to dispose those Parts into several Concords, as much as you can with convenience.

§ 6. *Concerning the Consecution of Perfects of the same kind; and of other Disallowances in Composition.*

I Told you *(pag. 32.)* that Perfects of the same kind, as two 5*ths.* or two 8*ths.* rising or falling together, were not allowed in *Composition.* Also *(pag. 33, 34.)* I shewed some other passages, prohibited in few (that is to say, in two or three) Parts. Here I will give you the reason why such passages are not graceful in Musick : And first concerning the Consecution of 5*ths.* and 8*ths.*

These two are called *Perfect Concords;* not only because their Sound is more perfect, (or more perfectly

Figurate Descant.

fectly fixed) than that of the other Consonants which are subordinate to them, but also, because they arise from the first two Proportions that are found in Numbers, *viz.* an 8*th.* from *Dupla*, and a 5*th.* from *Sesquialtera*, as I shewed *pag.* 79, and 80.

Now, as to the Disallowance of their following one another of the same kind; you may observe, that our Senses are still delighted with variety; as we may instance in this: Suppose an excellent Dish of Meat, prepared with greatest industry to please the Tast, were set before us to feed on, would it not be more acceptable to have some variety after it, than to have the same over again? The very same it is in Sounds presented to our Ear, for, no man that hath skill in Musick, can hear two perfect 5*ths.* or two 8*ths*, betwixt the same Parts, rising or falling together, but his Ear will be displeased with the latter of them; because he expected in place thereof some other Concord.

This Reason against the Consecution of 5*ths.* and 8*ths.* being admitted, we will now proceed to the other Disallowances; which, upon due examination, we shall find to arise from the very same consequence.

For the better understanding of This, you must know, First, that every Disallowance doth end either in an 8*th.* or in a 5*th.* (by these I also mean their *Octaves.*) Secondly, that a Disallowance is commonly generated by both the Parts moving the same way. Thirdly, that every Leap in Musick doth imply a transition by degrees, from the former to the latter Note, by which the Leap is formed. Lastly, that those implicit Degrees (by reason of both Parts moving the same way) do always produce a Consecution of two (if not more) Perfects of the same kind.

To

A Compendium of Musick.

To render this more clear, we will take some of those Passages not allowed in *pag.* 34. and break the Leaps into Degres, according to what I shewed *pag.* 51, 52. *of breaking a Note*, as you see in the following Examples:

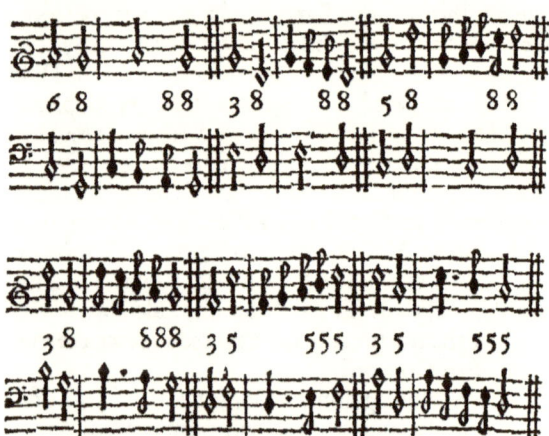

By this you see, that if both the Parts move the same way, one of them by a Degree, the other by a Leap; that Leap (I say) being broken into Degrees, begets a Consecution of two Perfects of the same kind: And where both Parts Leap the same way, if you break those Leaps into Degrees, there will arise from those Degrees, Three of the same Perfects. And this implicit Consecution of 8*ths*. and 5*ths*. arising from those Degrees, is that which renders such Passages less pleasing to the Ear, and are thereupon named *Disallowances*.

These which I have shewed may serve for your understanding of the rest, for they are all of the same nature, excepting One, which Mr. *Morley* and

Figurate Descant.

and others call *hitting an 8th on the face*; that is, when an upper Part, meeting the *Bass* upon an 8*th*. doth skip up from thence into some other Perfect Concord, thus.

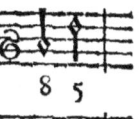

But whereas I told you, and have shewed, that a Disallowance is commonly generated by both Parts moving the same way, you must know, that all Passages of that sort are not Disallowances; for, you will hardly find a Disallowance where the Treble removes but one Degree; except that which I shewed in the first instance of the late Examples, where the Treble falls by a Degree from a 6*th*. to an 8*th*. or (perhaps) where the *Bass* shall make an extravagant Leap (as it were on set purpose) to meet the *Treble* in a 5*th*. or 8*th*. In any other way, I do not see how a Disallowance can occur, whilst the *Treble* removes but one Degree, though both Parts rise or fall together. But if the *Treble* or upper Part do skip, whilst the *Bass* removes but one Degree, (the same way) you may conclude it a Disallowance.

I will give you Examples of both these ways, that you may compare them by your Eye and Ear; and so you will better perceive what is, and what is not allowed.

Examples.

Passages into the 8*th*. Passages into the 5*th*.

Good. Bad. Good. Bad. Good. Bad. Good. Bad.

If you try the Sound of these two Ways with an Instrument, you will perceive that those Passages wherein the *Treble* removes but one Degree, are smooth and natural; but in the Other where the *Treble* doth Leap, the Passage is not so pleasing to the Ear.

The Reason whereof (as I conceive) is, because Leaps are the proper Movements of the *Bass*, and Degrees more natural to the *Treble* part, as I formerly delivered in *Plain Counterpoint*: And therefore, so long as both Parts proceed in their natural Movements (the *Bass* by Leaps, and the *Treble* by Degrees) the Consecution is not so perceptible, because it gives no offence to the Ear; for that which is proper and natural cannot be displeasing: But if you disorder' this natural Movement, by making the *Bass* to move by a Degree, and the *Treble* to Leap the same way into a Perfect Concord, the Consecution thereof presently begets a Disallowance.

Lastly, take notice, that most of those Passages we call *Disallowances*, may be tollerated in the *Tenor* or *Alt*, (being covered by a higher Part) though, in the highest Part, it self, they would not be allowable: And therefore when your *Treble* or highest Part shall make a Leap, (which is frequent in *Figurate Descant*) your chief care must be, that the said *Treble* or highest Part (compared with the *Bass*) be not guilty of any Disallowance; of which there can be no danger, if the Leap be made into an Imperfect Concord.

That you may better remember them, most *Disallowances* may be referred to these two Heads: 1. When the higher Part skips to a 5*th*. or 8*th*. whilst the *Bass* removes but one Degree. 2. When both Parts skip the same way into a 5*th*. or 8*th*. And this is as much as I think necessary concerning *Disallowances*.

§ 7. Con-

§ 7. *Concerning the Confecution of* 4ths. *and* 5ths.

I Formerly shewed you *(pag.* 74. *)* three different 4*ths*. *viz*. a *Lesser*, a *Greater*, and a *Middle* 4*th*. named *Diatessaron*, which for distinction I call a Perfect 4*th*. because it arises from the perfect dividing of an *Octave* into its 4*th*. and 5*th*. as well according to the *Arithmetical* as the *Harmonical Division* thereof.

These 4*ths*. are so necessary, (or rather unavoidable) in Composition, that you shall scarcely see Two, Three, or more Parts joyned to any *Bass*, but there will frequently be one of them betwixt some two of the upper Parts.

Again, Three Parts cannot Ascend or Descend together by Degrees in Musical Concordance, but there must (of necessity) be a Confecution of so many 4*ths*. betwixt some two of the upper Parts.

Now, if that Confecution consist of different 4*ths*. mixed one with another, it is very good: But if the 4*ths*. be of the same kind, the Confecution is not so allowable. The Reason thereof is, that 4*ths* are the Resemblances or Resonances of 5*ths*. as may be seen in This; that if you transpose the Parts which exhibit those 4*ths*. by placing the Lower an *Octave* higher, or setting the Higher an *Octave* lower, those 4*ths*. will be changed into 5*ths*: as you may see in the following Instances.

A Compendium of Musick.

Example.

Three 4ths. betwixt the Alt and Tenor. | Three 5ths. betwixt the Treble and Tenor.

The Notes transposed are those of the *Tenor* in the first Instance, which being placed an *Octave* higher, and so made the *Treble* or highest Part in the second Instance, begets three 5*ths*. instead of the former three 4*ths*.

The question now is, whether these three 5*ths*. being of different kinds, be not allowable in Composition. (If they be allowed, there is less doubt to be made of the 4*ths*. they being also different.) Here is no Consecution of Perfects of the same kind, for the middle 5*th*. is Imperfect: Neither is there any harshness or dissonance offered to the Ear, so near as I can perceive. And though Mr. *Morley* (in his *Introduction*, pag. 75.) with other precise Composers of former times, did not allow a Perfect and an Imperfect 5*th*. to follow immediately one the other; yet later Authors, as well Writers as Composers, do both use and approve it. See
Kircher,

Figurate Descant. 101

Kircher, in his *Musurgia Universalis*, pag. 621. *De licentia duarum Quintarum*, where he cites *Hieronimus Kapsperger*, a very excellent Author, using two 5ths. one after another, in divers places of a Madrigal, with much Art and Elegancy, and in the very beginning of the same, makes no scruple of setting four 5ths. *Perfect* and *Imperfect* one after another. The Example is this which follows.

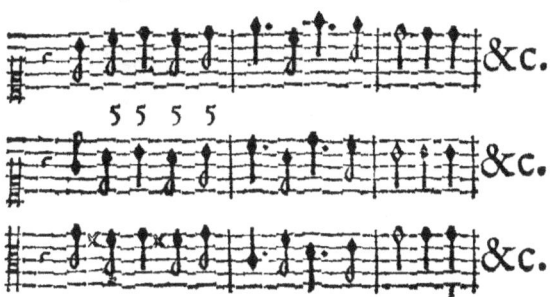

As for my own opinion, I do not only allow the Consecution of two 5ths. one of them being *Imperfect*, but (being rightly taken) esteem it amongst the Elegances of Figurate Descant.

This I speak, supposing them to be in short Notes. But if the Notes be long, as *Semibreves*, and sometimes also *Minims*, I should then rather choose to have the *Perfect* 5th. to hold on, till the other Part remove to a 6th. before it change to an *Imperfect* 5th.

As for Example.

Not thus,   but thus,   or thus,

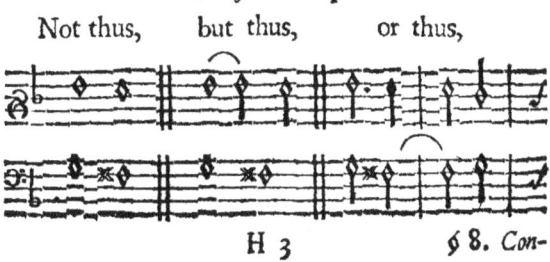

§ 8. Con-

§ 8. *Confecution of 3ds. and 6ths.*

TWo *Greater 3ds.* can hardly follow one the other, without *Relation* Inharmonical; yet in rising by degrees to a Binding Cadence they are allowable, as thus:

In which an Inner Part will properly come in, as you see in the Example.

And, by this you may perceive that

Relation Inharmonical is sometimes dispensed with; which must be referred (next after the Ear) to the judgment of the Composer.

Two *Lesser 3ds.* may follow one another in degrees, as thus:

But in Leaps they will not do so well.

Greater 6ths. are answerable to *Lesser 3ds.* and therefore may follow one another, as you may see next following:

Lesser 6ths, are like in nature to *Greater 3ds.* and therefore the Confecution of them is liable to Relation Inharmonical.

Thus you have a short account how *3ds.* and *6ths.*
may

Figurate Descant.

may follow one another when they are of the same kind. As for their change from *Greater* to *Lesser*, or the contrary, it is so natural, that you cannot Ascend or Descend, either in 3*ds* or 6*ths*. but it must be by a frequent changing from the *Lesser* to the *Greater*, or from the *Greater* to the *Lesser*.

Now, as to their Passage into other Concords; the most natural is commonly that which may be done with the least remove.

Hence it is observed, that the *Lesser 6th*. passes more naturally into a 5*th*. and the *Greater 6th*. into an 8*th*. as you shall see in the following Instances.

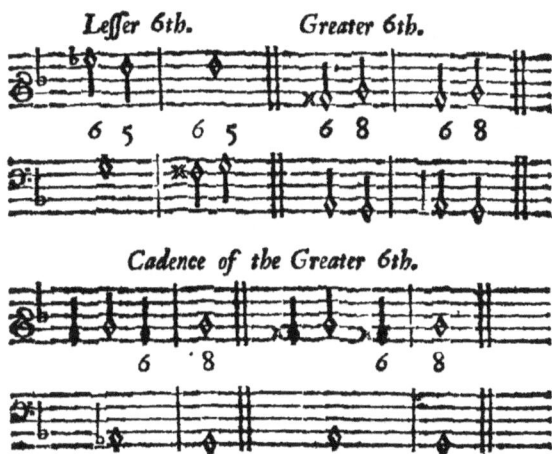

These little removes by a *Tone* or *Semitone*, do connect or make smooth the Aire of the Musick, in passing from Concord to Concord; which, by greater removes, would often seem disjoynted.

I will now speak of a Fuge, which is the prime Flower in Figurate Descant.

§ 9. Of Fuga *or* Fuge.

This is some Point, (as we term it in Musick) consisting of 4, 5, 6, or any other number of Notes; begun by some one single Part, and then seconded by a following Part, repeating the same, or such like Notes; sometimes in the *Unison* or *Octave*, but more commonly, and better, in a 4*th.* or 5*th.* above, or below the Leading Part.

Next comes in a Third Part, repeating the same Notes, commonly in an *Octave* or *Unison* to the Leading Part.

Then follows the Fourth Part, in resemblance to the second.

The Fifth, and Sixth Parts (if the Composition consist of so many) do follow or come in after the same manner, one after the other, the Leading Parts still flying before those that follow, and from thence it hath its name *Fuga* or Fuge. The Form of it you have in the following Example.

Example

Figurate Descant. 105

Example of a Fuge.

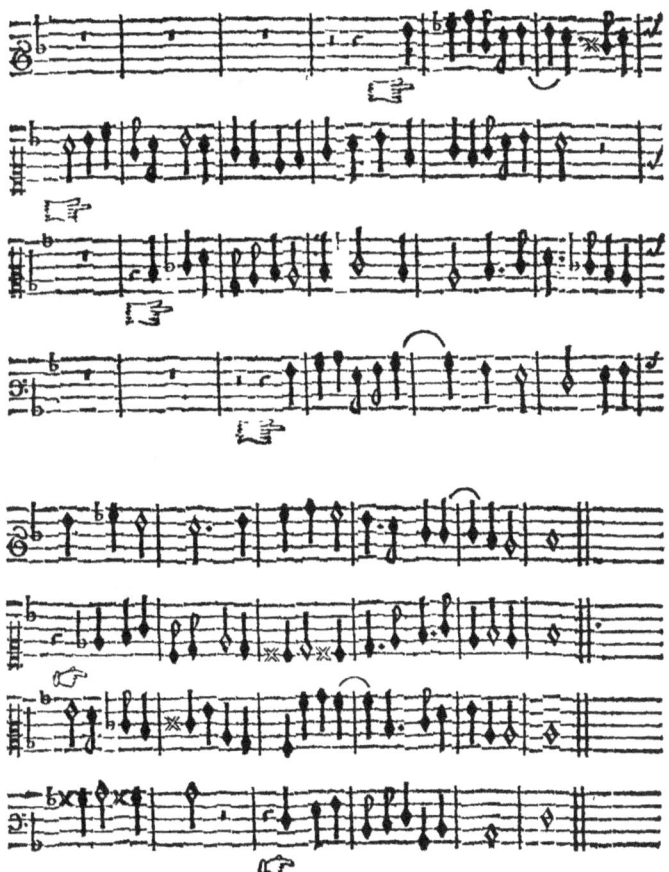

Here you may observe, that though the leading Part begins with an even Note, yet any following Part may come in upon an odd Note, with an odd Rest before it, when the Fuge doth require it, or permit it,

Like-

Likewise take notice, that you are not so strictly obliged to imitate the Notes of the leading Part, but that you may use a longer Note instead of a shorter, or the contrary, when occasion shall require. Also, you may rise or fall a 4*th.* or 5*th.* either instead of other; which is oftentimes requisite for better maintaining the Aire of the Musick.

§ 10. *Of* Arsin *and* Thesin.

Sometimes the Point is Inverted, or moves *per Arsin* and *Thesin,* (as they phrase it;) that is, where the Point rises in one Part, it falls in another, and likewise the contrary; which produces a pleasing variety: A Figure of it you may see in this Instance of the former Point.

Arsin.   *Thesin.*

An Example of it you have in that which follows.

Example

Figurate Descant. 107

Example of a Fuge per Arsin & Thesin.

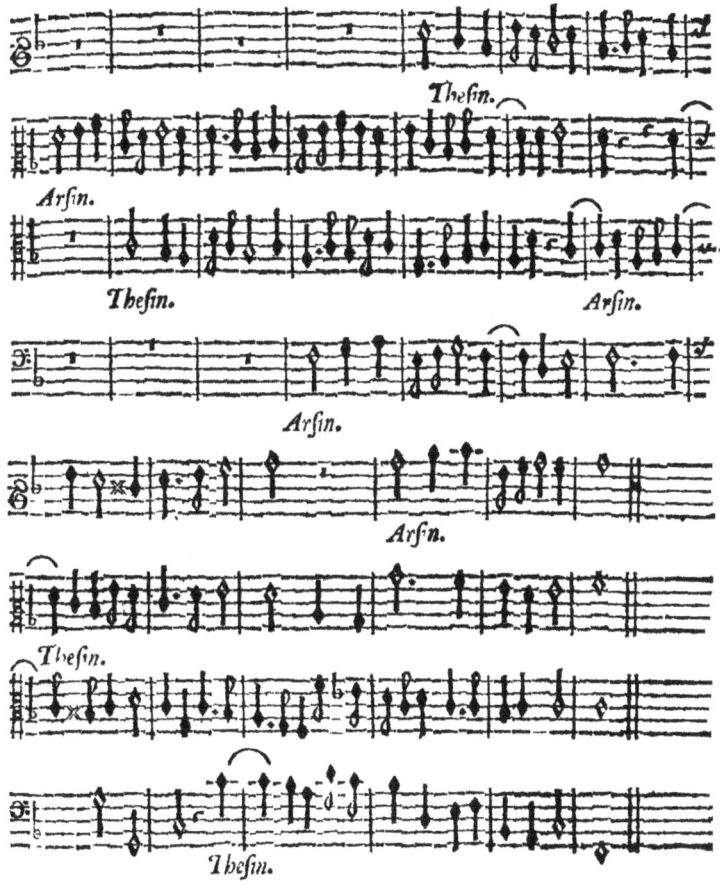

Thus you see the Point *per Arsin & Thesin,* so near as I could contrive it in so short an Example: only in the 7*th.* Bar, the *Tenor* doth not precisely express the Point; which I note unto you, as being
better

better (of the two) to injure the Point, than the Aire of the Musick, the design of a Composer being to please the Ear rather than to satisfie the Eye. Here the Point was exprest both ways in each Part, but it is left to your liberty whether you will have one Part maintain the Point *per Arsin*, another *per Thesin*, or what other way you shall think fit to mix them; every man being Master of his own fancy.

Sometimes the Point is Reverted, or turned backward thus:

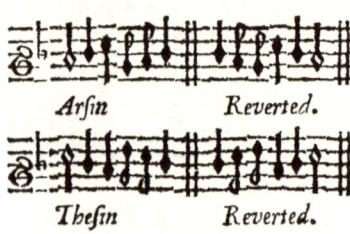

But then it must be such a Point as hath no Prick-note in it, because the Prick will stand upon the wrong side of the Note when the Point is reverted.

§ 11. *Of Double Fuges.*

SOmetimes the Musick begins with two or more different Points, which the Parts do interchange by turns, in such manner as they did in the late Inverted Fuge *per Arsin & Thesin*: An Example whereof you have as follows.

Example

Figurate Descant. 109

Example of two Points moving together in Fuge.

By these Examples you see what a Fuge is. I will now lead you towards the forming thereof, as Children are led when they learn to go.

§ 12. How

§ 12. *How to form a Fuge*

HAving made choice of such Notes as you think fit for your Point, Prick them down in that Part which you design to begin the Fuge.

That done, consider which Part you will have to follow next, and whether in a 4*th*. or 5*th*. above or below the leading Part. Perhaps the latter end of the Fuge Notes which you have Prickt down, may agree therewith. If not, you may add such other Notes as may aptly meet the following Part at its coming in.

Next, prick down the Fuge-Notes of that following Part; and add what other Notes may be requisite for meeting of the third Part, which (properly) will come in upon the *Octave* to the beginning of the leading Part.

Then carry on the third Part, by adding such Notes as may meet the beginning of the fourth Part, as it comes in upon an *Octave* to the beginning of the second Part. And, if you rightly conceive my words and meaning, your Scheme will appear like this which follows, according to the first Platform of our first Example of a single *Fuge*.

Example

Figurate Descant. 111

Example of the first Platform of a Fuge.

Having done this, you may fill up the empty places with such Concords and Bindings as you think fittest for carrying on your Composition; until you repeat the Fuge, in one of those Parts that begun it; which may be done either in the same, or in any other Key that will best maintain the Aire of the Musick; for good Aire is chiefly to be aimed at in all Musical Composition. And this repeating or renewing of the Fuge or Point, seems always more graceful when it comes in after some *Pause* or *Rest:* by which means more notice is taken of it; as of a man that begins to speak again, after some little time of silence.

The same method I have shewed in four Parts, may also serve you whether the Parts be more or fewer.

§ 13. *Of*

§ 13. *Of Musick Composed for Voices.*

THe ever renowned *Descartes*, in the beginning of his *Compendium of Musick*, insinuates, that, of all Sounds the Voice of Man is most grateful, because it holds the greatest conformity to our Spirits. And (no doubt) it is the best of Musick, if composed and expressed in *Perfection*.

More certain it is, that of all Musick, That ought to have the precedence which is designed to sing and sound forth the Praise and Glory of the Incomprehensible 𝕾𝖔𝖚𝖗𝖈𝖊, 𝕾𝖔𝖚𝖑, 𝕰𝖘𝖘𝖊𝖓𝖈𝖊, and 𝕬𝖚𝖙𝖍𝖔𝖗 of all created Harmony.

To this intent, *Hymns*, *Psalms*, *Anthems*, *Versicles*, *Responsaries*, *Motets*, &c. are set and Sung in Musick: of which no man is ignorant that hath frequented either the Churches beyond Sea, or the Cathedrals in *England*.

Of these forementioned, some are composed in Plain Counterpoint, others in Figurate Descant, with Points, Fuges, Syncope's, Mixtures of Discords, &c. according to what we have shewed and taught in this present Treatise.

In this divine use and application, Musick may challenge a preheminence above all the other Mathematick Sciences as being immediately imployed in the highest and noblest office that can be perform'd by Men or Angels.

Neither, in its civil use, doth it seem inferior to any of the rest, either for Art, Excellency, or Intricacy.

Whether we consider it in its *Theory* or *Mathematick* Part, which contemplates the Affections, Rations, and Proportions of Sounds, with all their nice and curious concernments.

Or in its *Practick* part, which designs, contrives, and

Figurate Descant. 113

and disposes those Sounds into so many strange and stupendious varieties, and all from the consequence of no more than three Concords, and some intervening Discords.

Or in its *Active*, or *Mechanick* Part, which midwifes and brings forth those Sounds; either by the excellent Modulation of the Voice, or by the exquisite dexterity of the Hand upon some Instrument; and thereby presents them to our Ear and Understanding; making such Impressions upon our Minds and Spirits, as produce those strange and admirable effects, recorded in History, and known by experience.

Any one of which three Parts of Musick, consider'd in it self, is a most excellent Art or Science. But this is a Subject might become a better Orator.

Of Vocal Musick made for the solace and civil delight of man, there are many different kinds, as namely, *Madrigals*, in which Fuges and all other Flowers of Figurate Musick are most frequent.

Of these you may see many Setts, of 3, 4, 5, and 6 Parts, published both by *English* and *Italian* Authors. Next, the *Dramatick* or *Recitative* Musick; which (as yet) is something a stranger to us here in *England*. Then, *Canzonets*, *Vilanella's*, *Airs of all sorts*, or what else Poetry hath contrived to be Sett and Sung in Musick. Lastly, *Canons* and *Catches*, (of which we shall speak hereafter) are commonly sett to words: The first, to such as be grave and serious: The latter, to words designed for Mirth and Recreation. Of these you may have Examples sufficient in a Book of *Catches* sold by Mr. *John Playford*, in the *Inner Temple*.

I § 14. *Of*

§ 14. *Of accommodating Notes to Words.*

When you compose Musick to Words, your chief endeavour must be, that your Notes do aptly express the sense and humour of them. If they be Grave and Serious, let your Musick be such also: If Light, Pleasant, or Lively, your Musick likewise must be suitable to them. Any passion of Love, Sorrow, Anguish, and the like, is aptly express'd by *Chromatick* Notes and Bindings. Anger, Courage, Revenge, *&c.* require a more strenuous and stirring movement. Cruel, Bitter, Harsh, may be exprest with a Discord, which, neverthelefs must be brought off according to the Rules of Composition. High, Above, Heaven, Ascend. as likewise their contraries, Low, Deep, Down, Hell, Descend, may be expressed by the Example of the Hand, which points upward when we speak of the one, and downward when we mention the other, the contrary to which would be absurd.

You must also have a respect to the Points of your Ditty, not using any remarkable *Pause* or *Rest*, until the words come to a full Point or Period. Neither may any *Rest*, how short soever, be interposed in the middle of a word, But a Sigh or Sobb is properly intimated by a *Crochet* or *Quaver Rest*.

Lastly, you ought not to apply several Notes, nor (indeed) any long Note, to a short Syllable, nor a short Note, to a Syllable that is long. Neither do I fancy the setting of many Notes to any one Syllable, (though much in fashion in former times;) but I would have your Musick to be such, that the words may be plainly understood.

§ 15. *Of*

§ 15. Of Musick design'd for Instruments.

WE must now speak a little more of Musick made for Instruments, in which, Points, Fuges, and all other Figures of Descant are in no less (if not in more) use than in Vocal Musick.

Of this kind, the chief and most excellent, for Art and Contrivance, are Fancies, of 6, 5, 4, and 3 Parts, intended commonly for Viols. In this sort of Musick the Composer (being not limited to words) doth imploy all his Art and Invention solely about the bringing in and carrying on of these Fuges, according to the Order and Method formerly shewed.

When he has tryed all the several ways which he thinks fit to be used therein; he takes some other Point, and does the like with it: or else, for variety, introduces some *Chromatick* Notes, with Bindings and Intermixtures of Discords; or, falls into some lighter Humour like a Madrigal, or what else his own fancy shall lead him to: but still concluding with something which hath Art and Excellency in it.

Of this sort you may see many Compositions made heretofore in *England* by *Alfonso Ferabosco, Coperario, Lupo, White, Ward, Mico,* Dr. *Colman,* and many more now deceased. Also by Mr. *Jenkins,* Mr. *Lock,* and divers other excellent men, Doctors and Batchelors in Musick, yet living.

This kind of Musick (the more is the pity) is now much neglected, by reason of the scarcity of Auditors that understand it. their Ears being better acquainted and more delighted with light and airy Musick.

The next in dignity after a Fancy, is a *Pavan*; which some derive from *Padua* in *Italy*; At first ordained for a grave and stately manner of Dancing, (as most Instrumental Musicks were in their several kinds, Fancies and Symphonies excepted) but now grown up to a height of Composition made only to delight the Ear.

A *Pavan*, (be it of 2, 3, 4, 5, or 6 Parts) doth commonly consist of three Strains; each Strain to be play'd twice over. Now, as to any piece of Musick that consists of Strains, take these following observations.

All Musick concludes in the Key of its Composition, which is known by the *Bass*, as hath been shewn. This Key hath always other Keys proper to it for middle Closes. (see *pag.* 36, 37.) If your *Pavan* (or what else) be of three Strains, the first Strain may end in the Key of the Composition, as the last doth: but the middle Strain must always end in the Key of a middle Close.

Sometimes the first Strain does end in a middle Close, and then the middle Strain must end in some other middle Close; for two Strains following immediately one another, ought not to end in the same Key. The reason thereof is obvious; to wit, the ending still in the same Key, doth reiterate the Aire too much; and different endings produce more variety. Therefore when there are but two Strains, let the first end in a middle Close that both Strains may not end alike.

I do confess I have been guilty my self of this particular fault (by the Example of others) in some things which I composed long since, but I willingly acknowledge my error, that others may avoid it.

Next

Figurate Descant.

Next in course after a *Pavan* follows a *Galiard*, consisting sometimes of two, and sometimes of three Strains. Concerning their Endings, I refer you to what was last said of a *Pavan*. This, (according to its name) is of a lofty and frolick movement. The Measure of it, always a *Tripla*, of three *Minims* to a Time.

An *Almane* (so called from the Country whence it came, as the former from *Gallia*) is always set in Common Time like a *Pavan*; but of a quicker and more airy movement. It commonly hath but two Strains, and therefore the first ought to end in a middle Key.

In these, and other airy Musicks of Strains, which now pass under the common name of Aires, you will often hear some touches of Points or Fuges, but not insisted upon, or continued, as in Fancy-Musick.

I need not enlarge my discourse to things so common in each ones Ears, as *Corants*, *Sarabands*, *Jiggs*, *Countrey-Dances*, &c. of which sorts, I have known some, who by a natural aptness and accustomed hearing of them would make such like (being untaught) though they had not so much Skill in Musick as to Prick them down in Notes.

Seeing this *Compendium* cannot contain Examples of all these which I give you account of, I would advise you to procure some, of such kinds as you most affect, and Prick them down in Score, one Part under another, as the Examples are set in this Book: that they may serve you as a Pattern to imitate.

But let them be of some of the best esteemed Composers in that kind of Musick.

You need not seek Outlandish Authors, especially for Instrumental Musick; no Nation (in my opinion) being equal to the *English* in that way; as well for their excellent, as their various and numerous Conforts, of 3, 4, 5, and 6 Parts, made properly for Inftruments; of all which (as I faid) *Fancies* are the Chief.

A

A COMPENDIUM OF PRACTICAL MUSICK.

THE FIFTH PART,

TEACHING The Contrivance of Canon.

§ 1. *Concerning Canon.*

A Canon is a Fuge, so bound up, or restrained, that the following Part or Parts must precisely repeat the same Notes, with the same degrees rising or falling, which were expressed by the Leading Part; and because it is tyed to so strict a Rule, it is thereupon called a *Canon*.

Divers of our Country-men have been excellent in this kind of Musick: but none (that I meet with) have publish'd any Instructions for making a Canon.

Mr. *Elway Bevin* professes fair, in the Title Page of his Book, and gives us many Examples of excellent and intricate Canons of divers forts, but not one word of Instruction how to make such like.

Mr. *Morley* in his *Introduction to Musick*, pag. 172. says thus: [*A Canon may be made in any distance comprehended within the reach of the Voice, as the* 3, 5, 6, 7, 8, 9, 10, 11, 12. *or other, but for the Composition of Canons no general Rule can be given, as that which is performed by plain sight, wherefore I will refer it to your own study to find out such Points as you shall think meetest to be followed, and to frame and make them fit for your Canon.*]

If, as Mr. *Morley* says, no general Rule can be given, our business must be to try what helps we can afford a Learner towards the making of a Canon. I am the more inclined to offer unto you this little Essay upon it, because the exercise thereof will much enable you in all other kinds of Composition; especially where any thing of Fuge is concerned, of which, it is the principal. And I will direct you in the same Method which I did before in contriving a single Fuge: that is, first, to set down your material Notes, and then, to accommodate your other Descant to those Notes.

§ 2. *Canon of two Parts.*

WE will, for more ease, begin with two Parts; and I will take the first two *Semibreves* of a former Fuge, to let you see the way and manner of it. The Canon shall be set in a 5*th.* above, and then your first Notes will stand thus:

Contrivance of Canon.

By 5*th*. 6*th*. 7*th*, &c. above or below is understood the distance of the Key betwixt the beginning Notes of either Part.

Having set down your beginning Notes, your next business is, to fill up that vacant space in the second Bar, with what Descant you please; which may be done in this manner.

Now, seeing that the following Part must also sing the same Notes in a 5*th*. above; it necessarily follows, that you must transfer the said new Notes, to the upper Part; and apply new Descant to Them also: and in this manner you are to proceed from Bar to Bar, still applying new Descant to the last removed Notes.

In this manner you may continue Two Parts in One, to what length you please. A short Example may suffice to let you see the way of it:

Example.

Take

122 *A Compendium of Musick.*

Take notice, that the Canon ends where you see the little Arches over either Part. The rest is only to make up the Conclusion, as we commonly do, unless we design the Parts to begin over again, and so to go round without a Conclusion.

In the foregoing Example the following Part came in above the other Part, we will now take a view of it coming in under the leading Part, and after a *Semibreve Rest*. The method is the same, only in This, we must remove the new added Descant downward, as before we carried it upward, still making new Descant to the last removed Notes.

Example.

Whether your following Part comes in after a *Semibreve* or *Minim Rest*, more or less, the method is the same, as you may see in this next following: In which, the lower Part comes in after a *Minim Rest*.

Example.

Contrivance of Canon. 123

Example.

Neither is there any more difficulty in setting your Canon a 7th. 9th. or any other distance either above or below, than in these which I have already shewed; as you may see by the next following sett in a 9th. above.

Example.

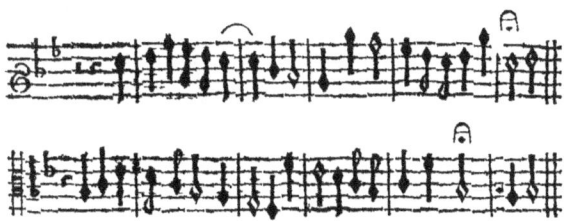

This, I suppose, is sufficient to let you see, with how much ease (being a little exercised in it) Two Parts in one may be carried on, to what length or shortness you please.

§ 3. *Ca-*

§ 3. *Canon of three Parts.*

WE will now make tryal of Three Parts in One, carryed on by the same Method. In which the Notes of the Leading Part must be removed upward or downward, according as the following Parts come in, either above or below the Leading Part.

I will first set down the Beginning Notes of each Part, as I formerly did of a single Fuge, that you may see the first Platform thereof, thus:

That being done; the first business is, to fill up the second Bar of the Leading Part, with some Note or Notes which may agree with that Part which came in next after it, and add the said Note or Notes to each of the other Parts in this manner:

Then fill up the third Bar of the Leading Part with some Note or Notes which may agree with both the other Parts, still adding the said Note or Notes to the other Parts. And thus you are to do from Bar to Bar.

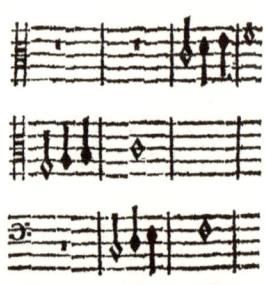

But if you perceive that your following Parts begin to run counter one upon another by these additional Notes, you must then try some other way; either by putting in a Rest, or by altering the course or Notes of the Leading Part: and in this particular
it

Contrivance of Canon. **125**

it is (as Mr. *Morley* said) that Canon is performed by plain sight.

Example of Three Parts in One.

If you would have your Canon to go round; the Conclusion must be omitted; and each Part must begin again, when it comes to that Note which is marked with a little Arch over it, where the Canon ends: and the Rests which are set at the beginning, before the following Parts, must be left out. And then the usual way of Pricking it down, is only the Leading Part, set alone, with marks directing where the other Parts come in, as follows:

a 3d. Canon in the 5th. below and 4th. above.

Hear me O Lord, and let my Cry come to thee.

§ 4. *Of*

A Compendium of Musick.

§ 4. *Of Canon in Unison.*

THe same Method might serve for a Canon in Unison: that is to say, The Leading Part must be accommodated to the following Part, when it comes in, and to both Parts when they sound together.

But I will give you a nearer Notion of it: In reference whereto, you may consider, that seeing each Part doth begin in the same Tone, it necessarily follows, that the foregoing Parts must move into the Concords of the said Tone; either Ascending or Descending, and by this means the Sound of the same Tone will be continued so long as the Parts move in the Concords of that Key.

As for example.

By this you see what Concords your Canon must move into, your care being no more than to avoid the Consecution of *Perfects* of the same kind, and to dispose your Parts (so much as you can) into different Concords.

Example

Contrivance of Canon.

Example of Canon in Unison.

§ 5. *Of Syncopated or Driving Canon.*

THere is another sort of Canon in Unison, in which the following Parts come in upon a *Crochet*, or upon a *Minim Rest*, one after another, and this kind of Canon may be applyed to any Ground or Plain-song consisting of *Semibreves*, or of *Breves*, if you double the length of the Descant-Notes.

I will first shew the way of it upon *Semibreves*, moving by degrees.

Example.

Example.

The Figures shew the Concords of the Leading Part to the Ground both Ascending and Descending. If the Ground consist of *Breves*, the length of the Descant Notes must be doubled. And this, I think may suffice, to let you see the order of your Descant, in those places where the Ground of Plain song shall rise or fall by degrees.

I will now let you see how to order your Descant when the Ground shall move by Leaps.

In which the movement of your Descant must be from 3*d.* to 3*d.* and your leading Part must also meet each Note of the Ground in a 3*d.* both which are easily effected, as you may see by the following Instances.

Contrivance of Canon.

Also, you have liberty to break a *Minim* into two *Crochets*, and to set one of them in an *Octave* above or below, when there shall be occasion for it.

You shall now see the former degrees and these leaps mixed one with another in this following Example:

A 4. Canon in Unison to a Ground.

130   *A Compendium of Musick.*

Here you see the Leading Part still beginning upon a 3*d.* to each Note of the Ground: Also a 6*th.* and 5*th.* following after the 3*d.* to meet the next Note of the *Bass* when it rises one degree, according to what was shewed in the Example of Degrees.

I will now set down this Canon in plain Notes, that you may better perceive, both the Syncopation, and also how the Parts move from 3*d.* to 3*d.* excepting where the *Bass* removes but one degree, in which places they make a leap to a 4*th.* Also you may observe, in the leading Part (and likewise those that follow) two places, where a *Minim* is broken into two *Crochets*, and one of them set an *Octave* lower, for better carrying on the Aire of the Descant, and keeping the Parts within due Compass.

Example.

We will try one Example more in this way, upon longer Notes of the Ground, the Descant Notes being made proportionate thereto.

A

Contrivance of Canon. 131

A 4. *Canon in Unison upon Breves.*

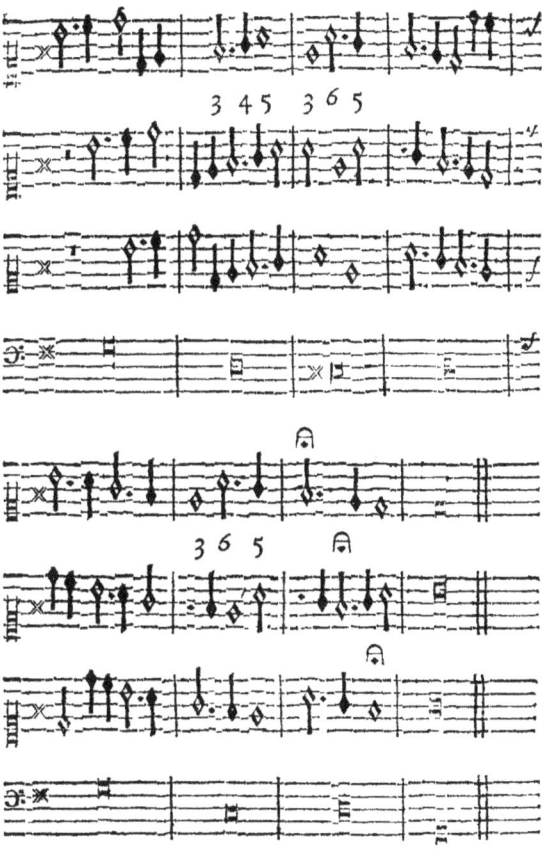

In these Syncopated Canons you may observe, that Two of the Parts do move up and down in an even Measure, and the other Part (by reason of its coming in upon an odd Rest) doth drive or break in betwixt them.

After the same manner of Syncopation or driving, Canons may be made (though not upon a Ground) the Parts being set a 4*th.* 5*th.* or 8*th.* one from another ; as you may see by these two following, made by the excellent Mr. *Matthew Lock,* Composer in ordinary to His Majesty.

A 3. *Canon in the* 8*th. and* 4*th. below.*

A 3. *Canon in the* 5*th. below and* 4*th. above.*

The Rule or Method of which is this; that the Parts (whether Ascending or Descending) proceed from 3*d.* to 3*d.* like the former two Canons in *Unison:* And break off to a 4*th.* the contrary way, to keep the Canon in due *decorum*; which otherwise, would Ascend or Descend beyond due limits.

The

Contrivance of Canon. 133

The position of the Parts, is according to the Harmonical Division of an *Octave*, which hath its 5*th.* in the lower place. The Driving Part is the *Sub-octave*, as you may perceive in their Examples.

§ 6. *Of Canon a Note Higher or Lower.*

Canon a Note Higher, is when each Part comes in a Tone or Note above another, as you may see in this next following; made by the forenamed Mr. *Mat. Lock* (to whom I do acknowledge my self much obliged, both for his suggestions and assistance in this Treatise.) This depends upon sight; and therefore no Rule to be given, excepting the helps formerly mentioned.

Canon a Note Higher.

Canon a Note Lower, is when the Parts come in a Tone or Note under each other; as you may see by the next following, made by our first proposed Method; with some little reference to sight.

K 3 *Example.*

Example.

Which may be Prickt in one single Part, and marked in manner as follows.

A 3. Canon a Note Lower.

Where Note, that the following Parts come in, as they stand in backward order, behind the Leading Part. And this is the best way of Marking a Canon, especially, when the following Parts come in upon several Keys, which may be known by the

several

Contrivance of Canon. 135

several Cliffs, which denote those Keys, and do also shew the compass of the Canon.

§ 7. *Of Canon Rising or Falling a Note.*

THere is another sort of Canon which Rises or Falls a Note, each time it is repeated, and may be composed by our first Method, only you must contrive it so, that it may end aptly for that purpose.

Example.

Canon Rising a Note each Repetition.

Canon Falling a Note each Repetition.

§ 8. *Of Retrograde Canon, or Canon* Recte & Retro.

SOme Canons are made to be Sung *Recte & Retro* (as they phrase it,) that is Forward and Backward, or one Part Forward and another Backward,

ward. Which may seem a great Mystery, and a business of much Intricacy, before one know the way of doing it: but that being known, it is the easiest of all sorts of Canons. This which follows shall serve for an Example of it.

Canon Recte & Retro.

Reverted thus.

Either of these alone, is a Canon of two Parts, one Part singing forward, the other, beginning at the wrong end, and singing the Notes backward. The Composition whereof is no more than this which follows.

Only the end of one Part, is joyned to the end of the other in a retrograde form, as upon examination you will easily find, if you look back upon the stroke which you see drawn through the middle of either. And after the same manner you may add more Parts to them if you please.

There is another way of Composing Musick to be play'd or sung forward and backward (much to the same effect) which is, by making the Parts double, as two *Trebles*, two *Basses*, &c. as you see here following.

Example.

Contrivance of Canon. 137

Example.

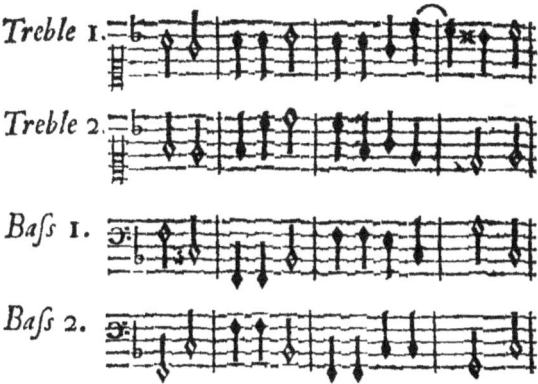

Here you have two *Trebles* and two *Basses*; which, as they now stand, may be played or sung, as well backward as forward, and will resemble a Lesson of two Strains: the first forward; and the second Strain backward; as upon trial you will perceive. But if you would have one Part to be sung Backward, whilst the other sings Forward; you must then turn one of the *Trebles*, and likewise one of the *Basses*, the contrary way, and joyn them together, so, that their two ends may meet in the middle of the Lesson, as you see in the following Example: and then the Harmony will be right, whether you sing them backward or forward, or one Part forward and the other Part backward. Likewise, Two may sing the *Treble*, one forward, the other backward, and other Two, the *Basse* in like manner, and then, it is a Canon of four Parts in two.

Example.

Example.

In like manner you may compose Six Parts in Three; or Eight Parts in Four, by adding two *Alts*, or two *Tenors*, or both; and then joyning their ends together, as we did these *Trebles* and *Basses*.

By this which hath been shewed, I suppose you see the way of Retrograde Descant. But I must advertise you, not to set any Notes with Pricks after them, in this way of *Recte & Retro*; because the Pricks, in the *Retro*, will stand on the wrong side of the Notes. Also, you must be wary how you use Discords therein, lest, in the *Revert* or *Retro*, they hit upon the beginning instead of the latter part of the Note.

§ 9. *Of Double Descant.*

IT is called Double Descant when the Parts are so contrived that the *Treble* may be made the *Bass*, and the *Bass* the *Treble*. I will give you an Example of it in Canon; *per Arsin & Thesin*, that (for brevity) I may comprise both under one, as in the Example next following.

Contrivance of Canon. 139

Double Descant on Canon per Arsin & Thesin.

This may seem a difficult business to one that is not very ready in his sight, but I shall render it as plain and easie as I did the first Examples of Two Parts in One, for it may be performed by the same Method. Only in this, you must invert the Notes as you place them in the following Part, accommodating your new Descant (Bar after Bar) to the Notes so inverted, as you may easily perceive by this Instance of its beginning.

But I must give you one Caveat, which is, that you must not use any 5*ths.* in this kind of Double Descant, unless in Passage or Binding like a Discord, because, when you change the Parts, making That the *Treble* which before was the *Bass* (which is called the Reply) those 5*ths.* will be changed into 4*ths.*

The

140   *A Compendium of Musick.*

The Reply.

The Canon begun in *Unison*; which, in the Reply, is changed into an *8th.* But the same Method serves in what distance soever it be set.

§ 10. *Of Canon to a Plain Song proposed.*

I Shewed you formerly how to Compose a Canon in *Unison* to any Ground of Plain-song consisting of *Semibreves* or *Breves*; and gave you Rules for it. But this which I am now to speak of, cannot be reduced to any Rule, (that I know) as depending meerly upon sight: and therefore, all we can do, is only to give you what help or assistance we are able, towards the effecting of it.

We will take (for Instance) one of Mr. *Elway Bevin*'s, not to be named without due praise for his excellent Book of Canons, Printed 1631. where you have Examples of Canons upon the same Plain-song, in all the distances contained in an *Octave*; of which this is one :

Contrivance of Canon. 141

Now, as to the Contrivance. First you are to consider, what Notes will serve your present purpose for the Leading Part, and also sute your following Part in reference to the next Note of the Plain-song. When you have found out Notes that will fit both these occasions, Prick them down; and then your beginning will stand in this manner,

Then you are to fill up the vacant Bar of the Leading Part, with such Notes as may also serve the following Part in reference to the next succeeding Note of the Plain-song, thus,

And in this manner you are to proceed, from Bar to Bar; still filling the empty Bar of the Leading Part with such Notes as may agree, both with the present Note of the Plain-song, and serve

serve the following Part for the next Note of the Plain-song also.

The same Method is to be observed though the Plain-song be placed betwixt, or above the other Parts. As also, whether your Canon be set in a 4th. 6th. 7th. 9th. or any other distance either above or below, as you may see by these two following Examples:

Canon in the 13th. below.

Canon in the 9th. above.

§ 11. Of

Contrivance of Canon. 143

§ 11. *Of Catch or Round.*

I Muſt not omit another ſort of Canon, in more requeſt and common uſe (though of leſs dignity) than all thoſe which we have mentioned; and that is, a Catch or Round: Some call it a Canon in *Uniſon*; or a Canon conſiſting of Periods. The contrivance whereof is not intricate: for, if you compoſe any ſhort Strain, of three or four Parts, ſetting them all within the ordinary compaſs of a Voice; and then place one Part at the end of another, in what order you pleaſe, ſo as they may aptly make one continued Tune; you have finiſhed a Catch:

Example.

Here you have the Parts as they are Compoſed; and next you ſhall have them ſet one at the end of another, with a Mark directing where the following Parts are to come in, as you ſee in this following Example.

144 *A Compendium of Musick.*

A Catch of Four Parts.

Having given you these Lights and Instructions for the Contrivance of Canon, which is the last, and (esteemed) the Intricatest Part of Composition; I must refer the Exercise of it, to your own Study and Industry.

And now I have delivered (though in brief) all such Instructions as I thought chiefly necessary for your Learning of *Practical Musick.* But it rests on your part to put them in practice: without which nothing can be effected. For, by Singing a man is made a Singer; and by Composing he becomes a Composer. 'Tis Practice that brings Experience; and Experience begets that Knowledge which improves all Arts and Sciences.

The End of the Compendium.

APPENDIX.

Short and Easie
AYRES
DESIGNED
For Learners.

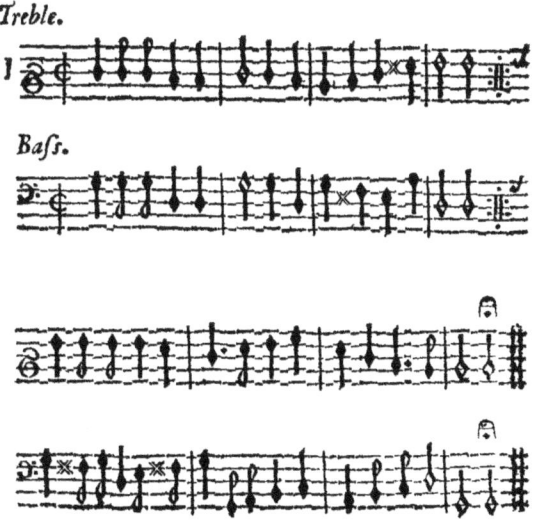

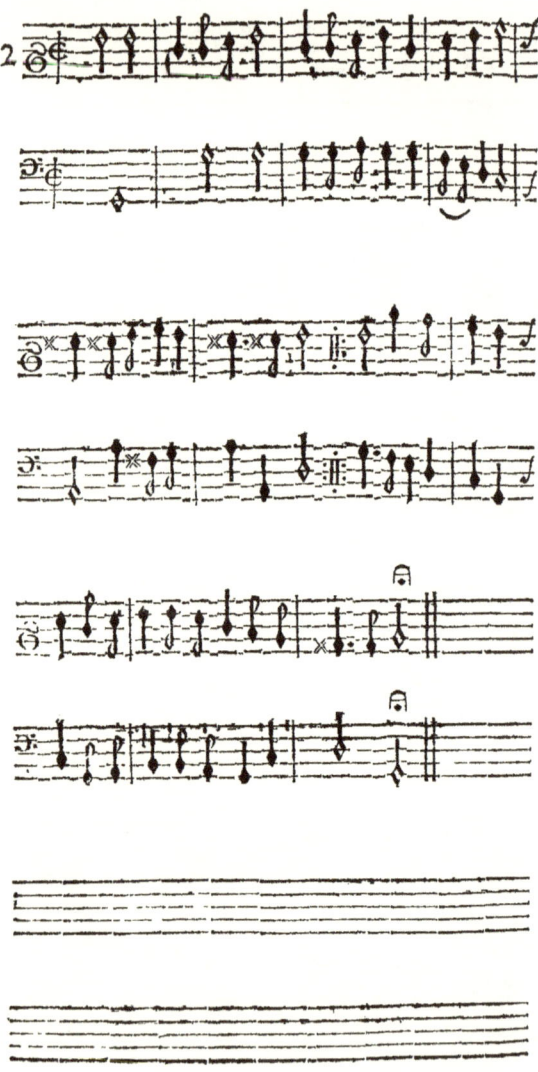

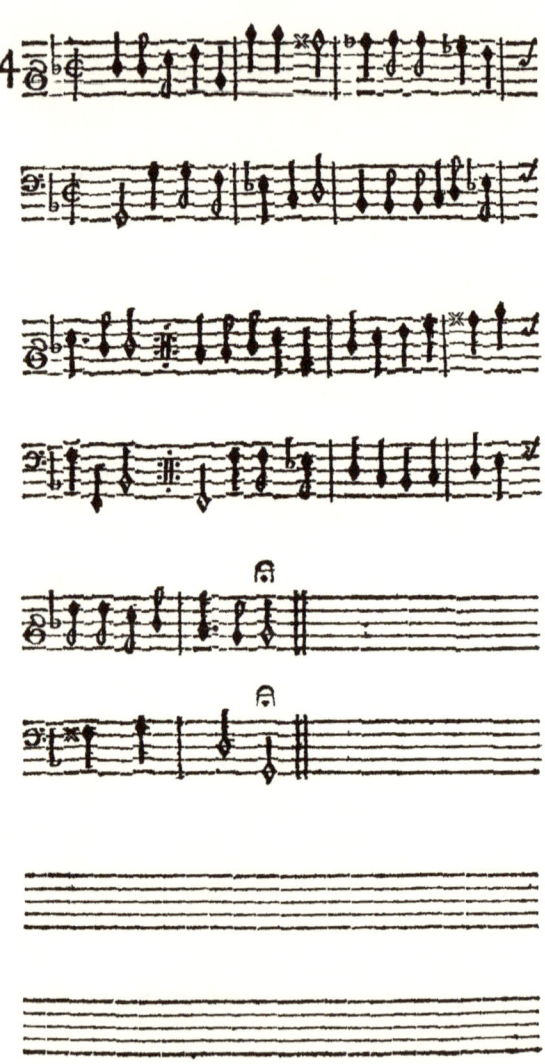

(150)

(151.)

(154)

(155)

12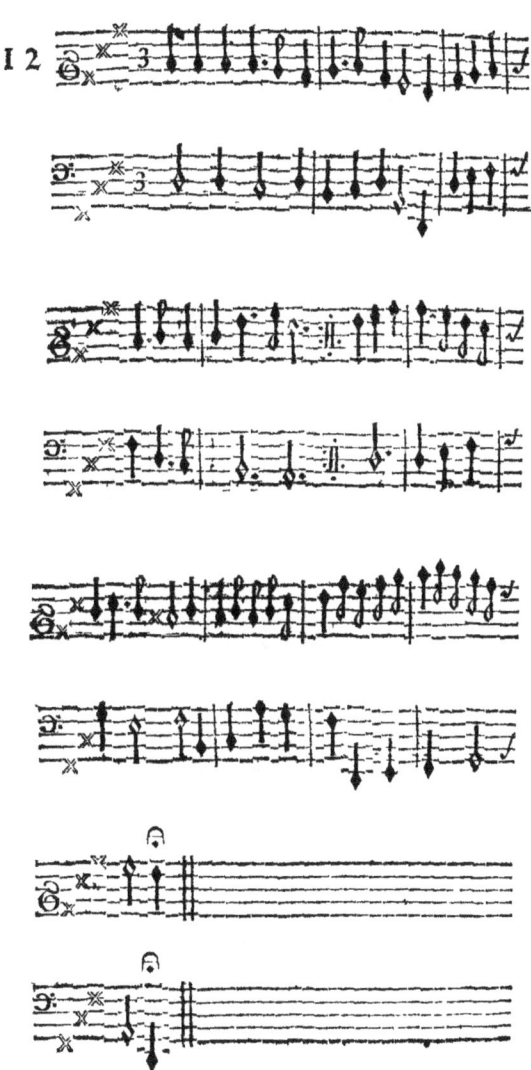

(160)

For two Bass-Viols.

(161)

For two Bass-Viols.

(162)

For two Bass-Viols.

(163)

For two Bass-Viols.

(164)

For two Bass-Viols.

Bass 1.

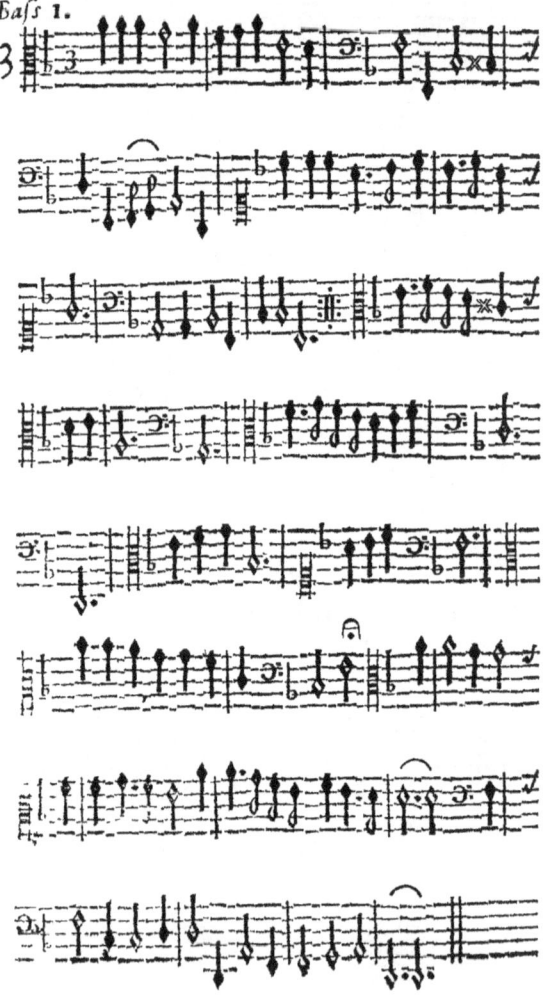

(165)

For two Bafs-Viols.

For two Bass-Viols.

Bass 1.

(168)

For two Bass Viols.

Bass I.

(170)

For two Bass-Viols.

Bass 1.

(171)

For two Bass-viols.

For Sir John St. Barbe, *Baronet*.

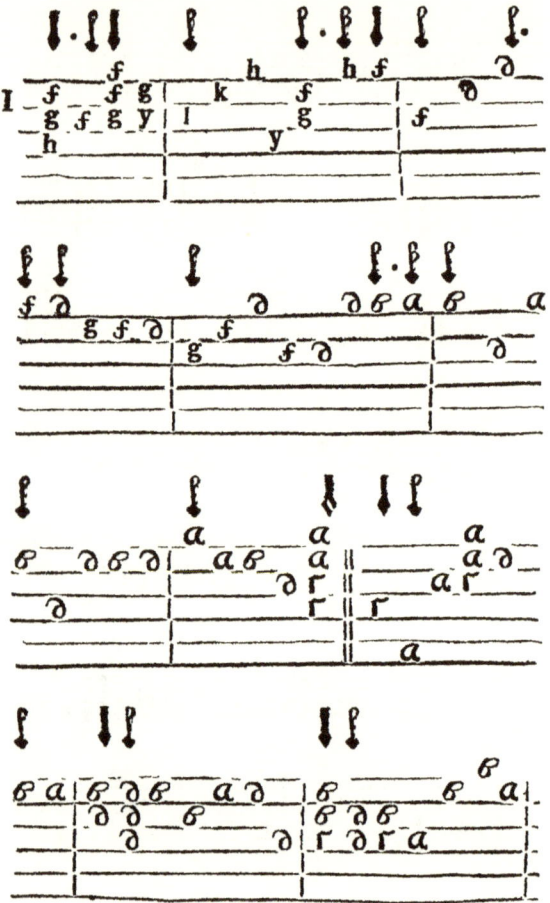

(173)

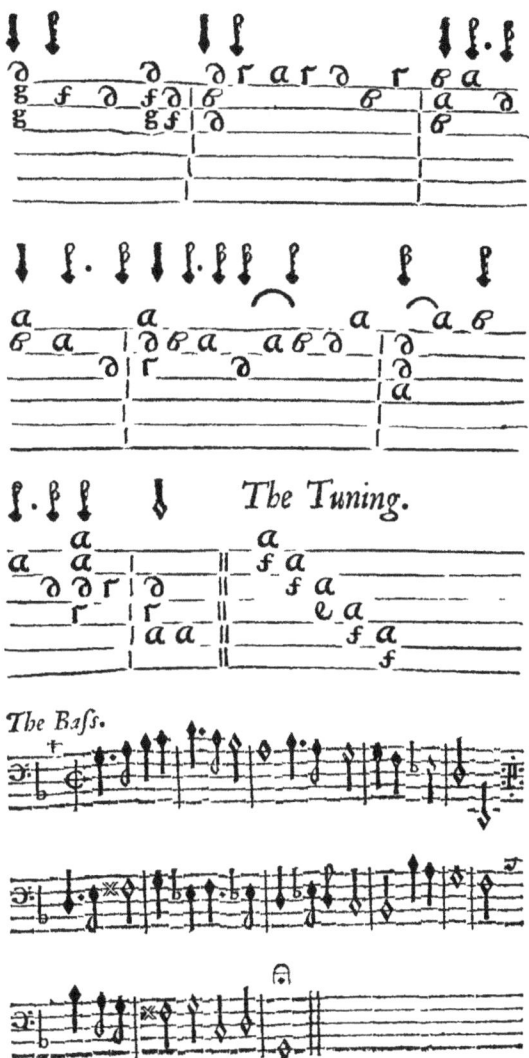

The Tuning.

The Bass.

(174)

(175)

The Tuning.

The Bass.

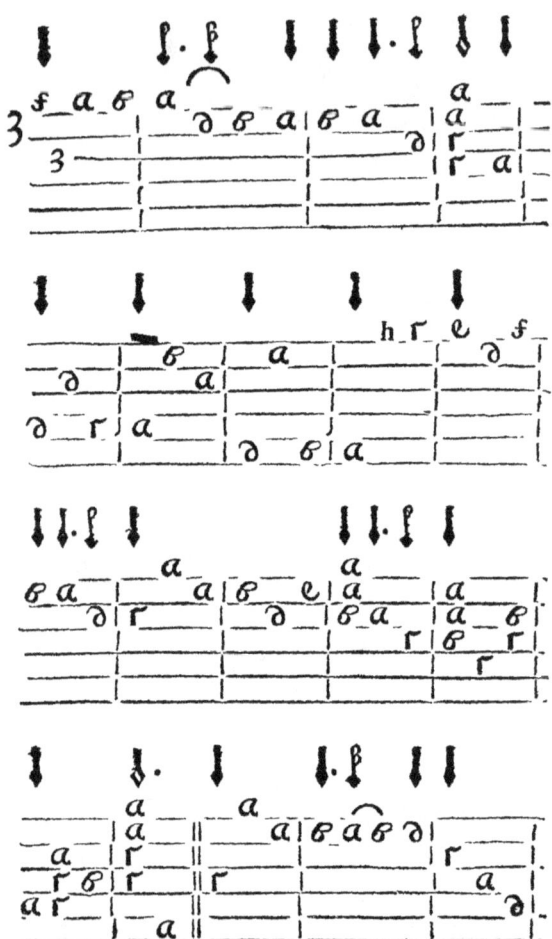

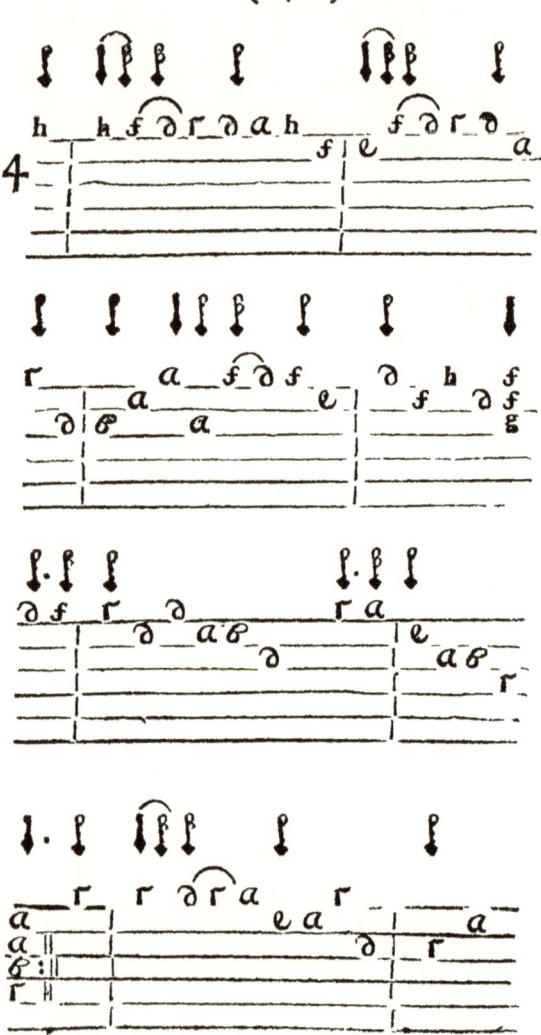

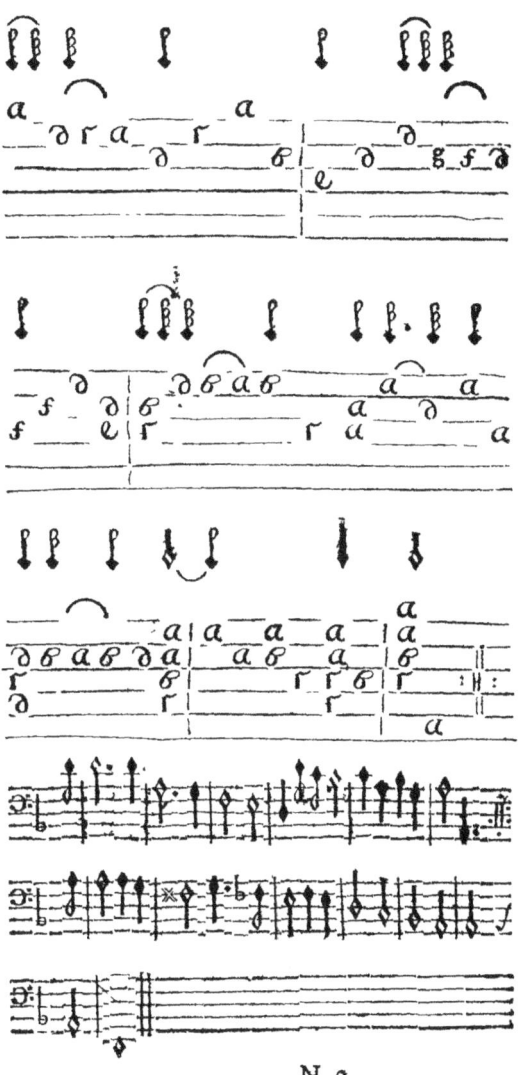

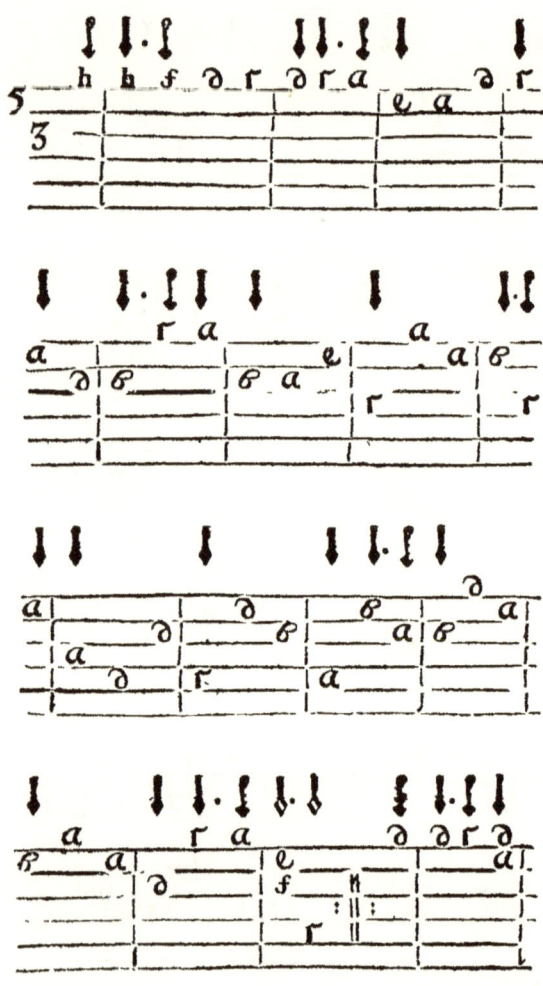

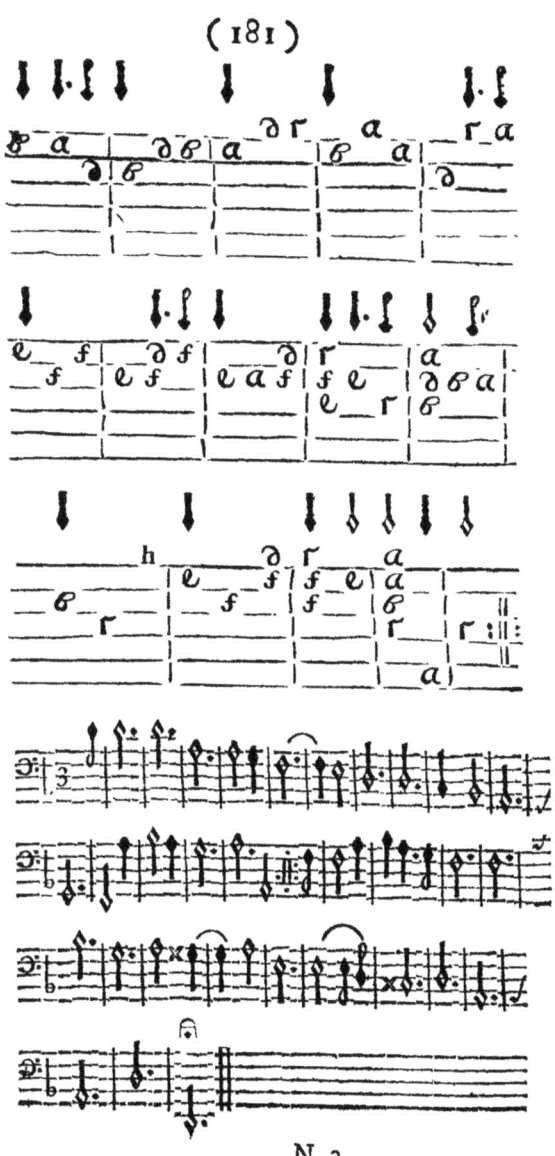

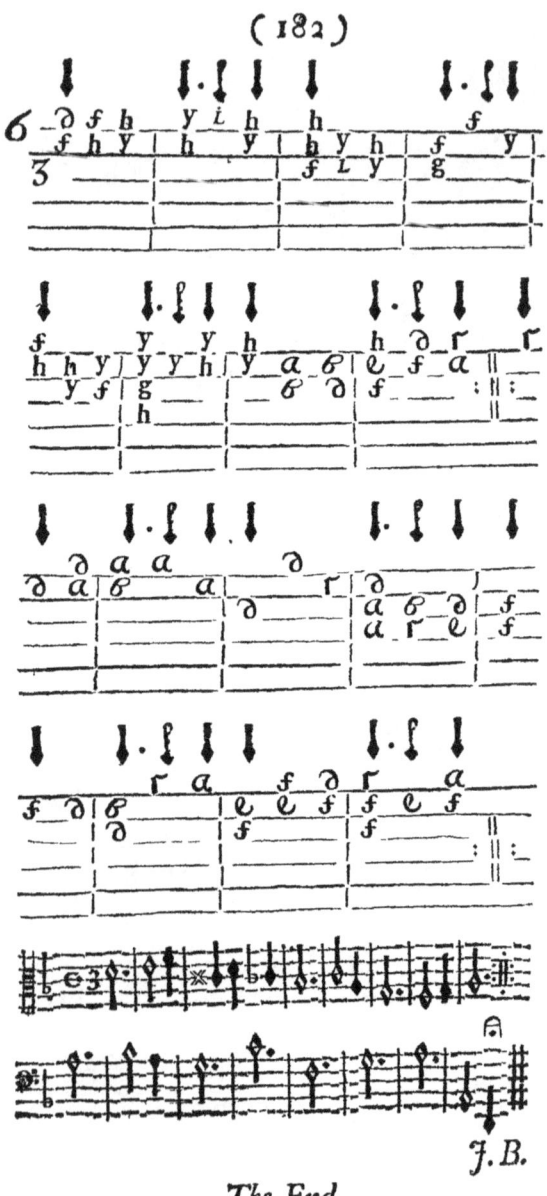

The End.

(183)

LESSONS by *sundry* Authors *for the* Treble, Bass-Viol, *and* Harp.

Francis Forcer.

(186)

Francis Forcer.

(188)

Two Parts.

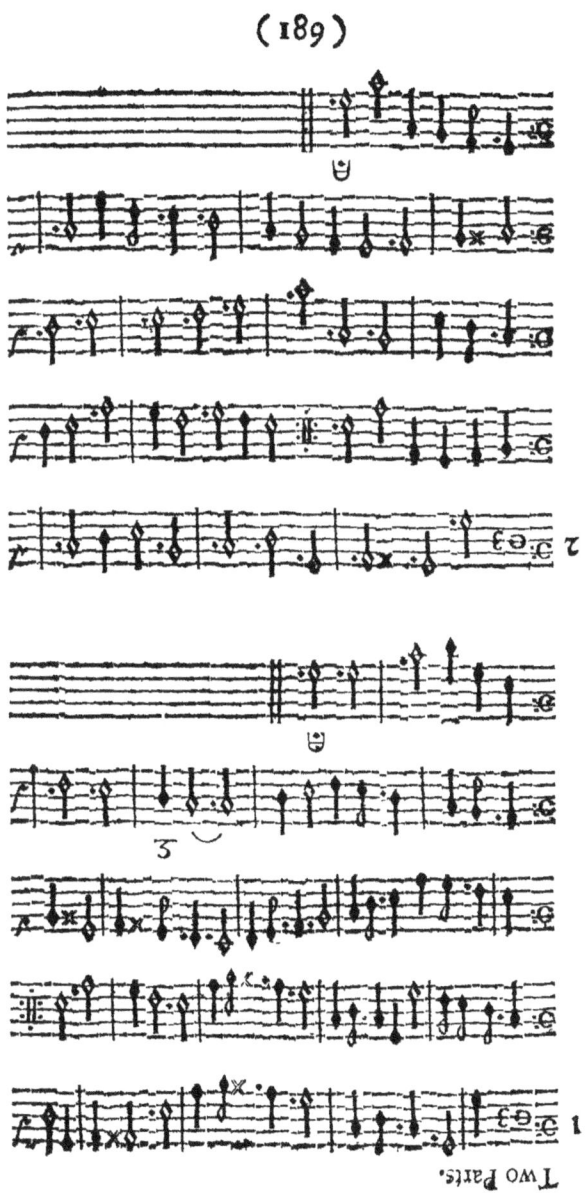

Two Parts.

Francis Forcer.

FINIS.

www.ingramcontent.com/pod-product-compliance
Lightning Source LLC
Chambersburg PA
CBHW032357040426
42451CB00006B/41